S0-BOI-485

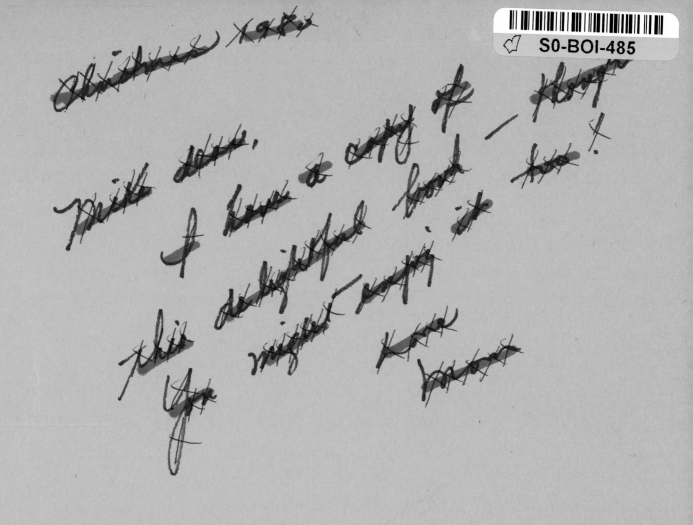

Longing for Darkness

Kamante's Tales

from Out of Africa

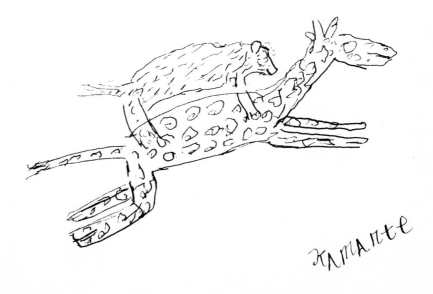

Harcourt Brace Jovanovich

LONGING FOR DARKNESS

With original photographs (January 1914 – July 1931)

KAMANTE'S TALES

and quotations from Isak Dinesen (Karen Blixen)

FROM OUT OF AFRICA

Collected by Peter Beard

New York and London

kinyegete

cheche

Copyright © 1975 by Peter Hill Beard

All rights reserved. No part of this publication may be reproduced or
transmitted in any form or by any means, electronic or mechanical, including photocopy, recording, or any information storage and retrieval
system, without permission in writing from the publisher.

Printed in the United States of America by Sidney Rapoport

Most of the opportunities for research and new material on Karen Blixen,
including photographs, were kindly provided by Thomas Dinesen. Through
Clara Svendsen and Tore Dinesen, access was gained to Det kongelige
Bibliotek and the private collection of Bror Blixen. Seventy-eight photographs are from the collection of The Rungstedlund Foundation and are
used with its permission. Thirty-six photographs from <u>The Life and Destiny
of Isak Dinesen</u>, by Clara Svendsen, collected and edited by Frans Lasson,
copyright © 1969 by Gyldendalske Boghandel, are reprinted by permission
of Random House, Inc. The quotations from Karen Blixen are from <u>Out of
Africa</u>, by Isak Dinesen, copyright 1937 by Random House, Inc., renewed
1965 by Rungstedlundfonden, and <u>Shadows on the Grass</u>, by Isak Dinesen,
copyright © 1960 by Isak Dinesen, and are reprinted by permission of
Random House, Inc.

Library of Congress Cataloging in Publication Data

Kamante.
Longing for darkness.

1. Tales, African.   2. Blixen, Karen, 1885-1962.
3. Country life—Kenya.   4. Aesopus. Fabulae.
I. Beard, Peter Hill, 1938-   II. Blixen, Karen,
   1885-1962. Out of Africa.   III. Title.
GR350.K25   398.2'09676'2   74-19092
         ISBN 0-15-153080-7

LAYOUT AND DESIGN: PETER BEARD AND MARVIN ISRAEL
EDITORIAL CONCEPTIONS: ALISON BOND

First Edition

B C D E

KAMANTE GATURA   KAREN

LANGATA

"We Nations of Europe, I thought, who do not fear to floodlight our own inmost mechanisms, are here turning the blazing lights of our civilization into dark eyes, fitly set like the eyes of doves by the rivers of waters (Song of Solomon 5:12), essentially different to ours. If for a long enough time we continue in this way to dazzle and blind the Africans, we may in the end bring upon them a longing for darkness, which will drive them into the gorges of their own, unknown mountains and their own, unknown minds."

Isak Dinesen.

Shadows on the Grass

A giraffe is so much a lady that one
refrains from thinking of her legs,
but remembers her as floating over

The plains in long garbs, draperies of morning mist and mirage.

Karen Blixen.

CONTENTS

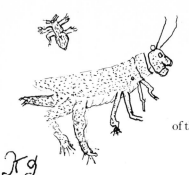

Xg

"All the time I felt the silent overshadowed existence
of the Natives running parallel with my own, on a different plane.
Echoes went from the one to the other."
—Isak Dinesen (Karen Blixen)

Twelve years ago last June, I made contact with Kamante Gatura through Ali Hassan and Juma's son Tumbo. These characters from Out of Africa sat, undated and alive, in the front seat of my Land-Rover as we drove from Nairobi to Rengute village in the Kikuyu Reserve. There we found Kamante, or Kamande (depending on how one pronounces the words of a language that was never written down). I presented him with a letter from Baroness Blixen and got a rumpled chicken in return. He then guided me to Mbogani House, or Karen Coffee Farm, in Karen, now a suburb. Kamante had not been back for over twenty years.

It was a case of "Open sesame" as he brought me through the doors of the dark paneled rooms, pointing out where Lulu the bushbuck had slept (saying that lulu is the Swahili word for "pearl"), the window where God was seen, the dining room where the old German clock sang out, an object of wonder in the African Highlands; the place where Minaba the owl perched in "Mrs. Karen's" office, the pantry and kitchen and the old stove on which he prepared recipe after recipe from the Sultans Cake Book. Here was where Pania and Dusk, the Scottish deerhounds, lay down at meals; here Farah Aden had stood, "straight...fine," "as decorous a figure as you would find anywhere... doorkeeper to all those years"; here Mr. Berkeley Cole and Mr. "Pinja-Hatern" traded stories between safaris; here, out on the porch, was where MacMillan's special chair was kept, and where the "Duke and Prince of Wales" sat sampling the "sauce of the pig."

We walked to the blind Dane Knudsen's place and from there to Mrs. Karen's brother "Mr. Thomas's" house, site of the shooting accident. Several hundred

KAMANTE'S KITCHEN

yards below, where the Mbagathi River turns to form a corner boundary of Karen Farm, lay the ruins of the old mill where the two Indians were murdered. (The great millstone into which their blood had seeped was then moved up behind the house by Mrs. Karen.)

Trees had grown forty feet through the back terrace stones on which aged Kikuyus had once squatted waiting for Msabu's artful prescriptions. But they were the same slabs of stone, and the events that had taken place on them came back to Kamante despite the years that divided him from them. It was a pleasure to see his unruffled fatalism as the old Africa took shape around him. His last picture in this book shows him standing against the Ngong Hills at the end of the day on which we began the recordings that have become Kamante's Tales from Out of Africa.

Over a period of twelve years, sometimes casually, sometimes scrupulously, and sometimes with grand propriety, as if divesting himself of his possessions, Kamante put down the extra dimensions of truth which are at the heart of Out of Africa. In Room 205 of the New Stanley Hotel in Nairobi, Abdullahi (from Shadows on the Grass), Saufe Aden (from Out of Africa), and I sat down with Kamante and three of his sons to make hundreds of hours of tape recordings in Swahili, translations, transcriptions, and editings. A few months ago, the final version was copied out by hand in ten days in the main tent of Wart Hog Ranch, the camp outside Nairobi where we had all come to live. On April 17, at the best hour of the day, under the eyes of two passing giraffes, a couple of dik-diks, and the incorrigible hogs, the last page was completed.

Farah Aden

SAUFE
ADEN

'Je responderay'

Denys Finch Hatton

Karen Blixen had always wanted Kenya to be given to the King of England as a personal present. In place of this delirious notion, which would have meant that no one would be taxed—for who can be taxed in paradise—her creditors forced her to leave the country, her closest friends died, or were killed, or killed themselves. After seventeen years, she had to say good-bye to her life in Ngong, and in July 1931 she sailed, broken, for Europe, with an advanced case of malarial jaundice, in a third-class deck space on the SS Mantola. She was leaving behind an Africa littered with the graves of her friends. Over a million dollars of family capital had been lost in her dream; the Karen Coffee Farm had come to grief through years of drought, disease, locust hordes, and cold high-altitude winds spilling over the Ngongs.

Her younger brother, Thomas Dinesen, who had given up his own ranching schemes in East Africa to support her, went out to meet the ship at Marseilles on August 19 and take her back to Denmark. There she vanished into her father's sepulchral attic at Rungstedlund, from which, it is not too much of an exaggeration to say, she did not emerge until she was published in America and selected by the Book-of-the-Month Club.

It took Karen Blixen twelve years to bring herself to unpack the wooden crates—of books and mementos—which she, Kamante, and Farah had packed up at Ngong in that sad, vestigial summer of 1931, crates on which she and Denys Finch-Hatton had sat and dined after the farm and the horses were sold, the furniture dispersed, and Dinah and David, grandchildren of Dusk, given away to friends.

In the stunning silence of those years she wrote her way out of a living death, created a tapestry of prodigious adventure out of the proud landscape in the Pleistocene in which friends and natives and animals alike fanned out beside her, in the

Ali bin Hassan

PARAMOUNT CHIEF
KINANTUI

haze of myth. "Navigare necesse est—vivere non necesse" was Karen Blixen's first motto. "This too shall pass" was her last.

When she died in September 1962 at Rungstedlund, in the house where she was born, Kamante wrote to me, 3,000 miles away, where I was working on a book she had helped me to construct, The End of the Game:

> "I was deeply shocked to learn the death of my everlasting dear Baroness Blixen and I whole heartedly shared this sad with you and the rest friends. Had I been in any ancestral power I could keep her immortal as my dear parent. I share the prayer with you and friends to keep her in the paradise where we shall meet her in that beautiful shore where all human sits in peaceful rest. I am beyond the happiness for this message you suddenly sent me. The kind deeds I was receiving from her are untold and the old life we stayed with her, like black and white keys of a piano how they are played and produce melodious verses. . . ."

Within the year her close friends "Cape to Cairo" Grogan and J. A. Hunter also died, and her former husband's safari partner, Philip Percival, who took Teddy Roosevelt out in 1909, and Pop Binks, Nairobi's oldest resident, who had made the early photographs of her and her household. All of them knew how little impact they had had on the endless bush country they had pioneered.

1915 BROR AND KAREN BLIXEN

ISAK + THOMAS DINESEN at his house 1921

MASAI CHIEF SENDEYO and wife

JUMA'S CHILDREN

"There is something vexatious and mortifying" in the fact that the natives "know nothing of gratitude . . . and what you do disappears, and will never be heard of again. . . . It is an alarming quality; it seems to annul your existence as an individual human being, and to inflict upon you a rôle not of your own choosing . . . as if you were the weather."

In the Africa of Karen Blixen and her friends this was accepted, for in wilderness no one expects recognition. Yet in the same way that Lulu had been coaxed to share the wilds with the people inside Karen House, so had Kamante learned to move between two worlds. Years after she left Africa, he was able to write her:

"Write and tell us if you turn. We think you turn. Because why? We think that you shall never can forget us. Because why? We think you remembered still all our face and our mother names."

It was Kamante she had relied on, time and again, to make his way by torch through the forest night to Mr. Thomas's small house and lead him to where she lay tormented by uncertainties. Time and again, he would offer reassurances until she could sleep; and in the morning she would wake to see the world in its accustomed height. As Thomas Dinesen writes:

the farm was financially in some difficulties when I went out —
after two very bad harvests I lost most of my faith in our farm and left Kenya
worn down and frustrated.
But long after I had gone she stayed on,
trying I suppose to hear an echo from
that isolated darkness that was
really then Africa.

Here, so many years later, is Kamante's book in response to her longing: not only his memories of her, but also the animal and human fables she had always hoped to translate into Swahili. The selection at the end blends Aesop's fables with African folk tales, but they contain the same truth: "When you have caught the rhythm of Africa, you find that it is the same in all her music."

Karen Blixen's vigil on the farm was sustained by her determination to find the truths she felt Africa "amongst the continents" could reveal. In that rarefied land "distilled up through six thousand feet" and millions of years, "dry and burnt, like the colours in pottery," or lush and green from the rains, she experienced great losses and great gains. After seventeen years of struggle, like the person in "From an Immigrant's Notebook" who awoke from a nightmare to see the beautiful stork his footprints had made sleepwalking in the earth, she turned loss and confusion into art. Out of Africa bloomed like a flower from a corpse. Now, more than forty years later, white and green flowers grow from the millstone that she considered the center of her farm.

In Last Tales she wrote: "Where the story-teller is loyal, eternally and unswervingly loyal to the story, there, in the end, silence will speak."

And so Kamante begins: "I was cooker in her house . . ."—Kamante of whom she had written: "He had no gift whatever for admiration." She was wrong.

Hog Ranch
Box 4191 Nairobi
April 1974

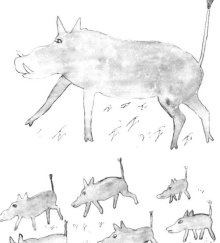

"O sacred sorrow, mother of all joy —
yearning to happiness, night to morning yields.
--- Light comes from darkness, daybreak comes from night."
                    Karen Dinesen
                         1905

Perhaps it was the darkness, the silence and the stars
which sometimes induced her to talk, as if she had
been quite alone, about her own views upon life, her
own visions for the future, her dreams and hopes, —
how passionately she craved to become part of the great,
the beautiful world, how desperately she longed for
wings to carry her away —
        I did not quite catch on to her ardent words
then, — how could I? — and not until much later did I
understand, with full sympathy, that her happy home-
life, with her sisters and brothers, with every care for
her welfare taken, with love from every side, might not
always be easy to endure, — her very love for her home
could turn out to be an unendurable shackle, fetter-
ring her wings —
        Little did she realize how much it would
cost to fly away — the price of her genius and her
"joy" in Africa.
                    Thomas Dinesen
                         1974.

To Kamante

I shall never forget our years together, and I shall look forward with great pleasure and expectations to your book

Your old friend
Thomas Dinesen

Thomas Dinesen
on the Lewis Glacier
Mount Kenya, July 1922

MY BACK HISTORY

CHAPTER I

In which Kamande Gatura and family move …
the boys' quarrel … death of the goat …
Mrs. Karen's shamba

"There is no world without Nairobi's streets."

Approaching the New Stanley Hotel, along Delamere Avenue

KAMANDE
GATURA
1921

Chapter I

MY BACK HISTORY

I, Kamande Gatura, was cooker in her house.
During that Life with Mrs. Karen I did drive
to Nairobi by way of Muthaiga and compete
with the best other cooks, going to the
Norfolk Hotel, the Stanley, and the Tors
Hotel, and the other called Queens Hotel.
We travelled the Ngong road way. By then
there wernt very many constructions as there
are now. We could sleep in Nairobi.
Mrs. Karen had Lots of welcome friends.

The first person to go to Mr. and Mrs.
Barance Blixen to inquire for a _shamba_ — a farming garden

"They very likely regarded me as a sort of superior squatter on their estates."

was my father by accidents. He first went
to chief Kinyanjui and said that we were
going to Ngambaru's, Shamba. But the shamba
we were going to was of Mrs. Karen. We
reached after a long journey from our
old Njakaï farm. And it passed like
this:

My father was one of the elders who
used to meet at every case of the Kikuyu
paramount chief, Kinyanjui. Chief could not
hold any meeting without my father's presence.
With the other Mzees (elders) he was well
respected and by chief himself. There
could be sometimes cases as far as Nyeri
and they would all go. Then chief did select
some Wazees (many elders) with leadership like my
father to go and settle everything there.
But there was one brother of chief Kinyanjui
who was called Kimotho. Kimotho had
married my step sister called Wahu
Gatura, the families becoming all close. There was
one older brother of mine called Njuguna
Gatura; and a son of Kinyanjui (now my brother
by Law) called Muthama. They were of the
same age and could go drink together.

They once did drunk and Muthama abused my brother. They quarelled in our home. My brother grew angry and asked "Why have you abused me in front of my father and young children and mothers?" He continued, "you could have waited until they were away from home." All disapointed, he asked Muthama whether he was abusing because his father was the chief or what... Muthama never stopped to give insults. So my brother Njuguna grew hot, and took out his knife and cut him by the neck and back, and even by his legs severly.

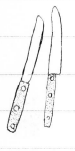

My father was very sorrowful because of this deadly action. He said, "I am one of the chief's councilors. I think chief Kinyanjui is going to detest myself." He said that he was going to shift me, Kamande, and my brothers Kiguru and Wakaba to become farther away. Njuguna got left alone with his mother because he

Kamante

was so quarellsome.   And my
father himself did flee.   He
told us to open our shamba and let every
sheep and goat out.   Kiguru and I
were to lead that herd and him
and Wakaba to push behind.   We
left the home and set out for our
journey that got announced as
Ngambaru's shamba.

   We reached at a certain place known
as Rirota.   One goat was very fat and unable
to walk.   We pushed intil the edge of the
forest to a fig three known as Mugumo wa
Njuguma

   There that goat died.   My father asked
a knife to slaughter. I myself was driving the
herd.   The meat was tied with its skin and
some leaves of the forest and we set off from
the Mugumo.   That very Mugumo is the one
used by all Kikuyu young fellows for
throwing clubs as to be known
who is stronger and best.

   We went until the other side of
the forest reaching a certain
house of a European known as

Mr Ree. We left the way to Ngong and followed the small road to Karen House then called "Bogani" (BUSH). We children never knew where we were. We met people whom my father knew and he said to make fire places. people of the farm were asked to came and stay with us for Lions or Leopards could come and kill the goat at night. We burnt our meat and shared with everybody ~~there~~. Thus we were by accidents at Karen farm.

And the very shamba we were going all the time was of Mrs. Barance Blixen. We had no hause but our goats had somewhere to spend ~~kill~~ the nights for we erected one small boma made of bushes. We made three big fire places with many firewoods and nobody slept the whole night. We kept on looking at the goat in fear of the Lion.

Our job was then to cut down trees. We were told to take care against reptiles and even Lions. Our father told us that the meat we had carried wouldn't be roasted all. We were to roast ribs

and the rest to be boiled.   Our

mother was far away in our old shamba

and we had no one to care for us   so we

had to preserve the meat very much.

My father had six wives but he said only

four will come with him.   The rest two will

be left in our old homes for their children

were very quarrellsome.   He said that he

who will make troubles as quarrells will

shortly be taken to prison.   Murigi,   my mother,

and Nduta my sister were also to be working

in the shamba of Mrs. Karen.   My father said

that these two women will work for three

months then be replaced by some others from

our shamba.   We were a big family and

that's how we were divided and switched.

my FATHER

"They had deep roots to their nature as well, down in the soil and back in the past . . .
which, like all roots, demanded darkness."

My father went to Mrs. Karen and asked her
whether he could bring his cows with him
for milk. She agreed but the manager
Deakson was to refuse. Mrs. Karen said
the cattle should come to give children
milk. The cows were brought by my father
and a certain Mzee known as Watenga I
myself was there then.

Kikuyus behind the house

MRS KAREN
1921

DUSK

We stayed nearly the first World War. The farm seemed as if it were ours. There occurred an epidemic of coughing. My father started to have this disease of coughing. He died from this and we started to separate as then there wasn't anybody responsible for our home. Every boy took his mother to where he wanted. You know when a father of a home dies, every child does what he wants.

The dining room

Mr. Thomas Dinesen, younger brother

MRS KAREN, MANAGER, MR BROR AND FARAH 1914

ñganga

Karen
Blixen

Rashidi bin
JUMA

First picture of the household sent to Europe

Abdullahi

Mohamoud
Noor

Njoroge
Wachegi

arah.

Said bin
Bekar

a visiting friend
of Farah's

MY SICK LEG

CHAPTER 2

A disease of the leg … I meet fierce dogs …
tied up with medicine …
staying at Mission hospital …
my cooking duties

"Small figures in an immense scenery"

"I came upon him for the first time one day when I was riding across the plain
of the farm, and he was herding his people's goats there."

CHAPTER 2

MY SICK LEG

After the death of my father I myself got a very serious disease, a fatal wound of the Leg. No medicine could I get, people were only bringing me native drugs from the forest. I couldn't go from my home.

There was one Luo called Oyamo who had carried off my hen saying he would bring me six shillings at the month's end. No promised Luo appeared. After a long season, I went to where he was working making silks for dresses and asked him about my money. He told me that he had spent his money on some other interests. I was helpless.

Now, if I could receive that amount of mine, I could then walk slowly up to Kikuyu Mission Hospital and be treated. When my mother went to work I was left alone with no one to help me.

I was going to be wise and report that Luo to the shamba manager. I went on my way with a stake for walking. Going I met with the European, Deakson.

I told him that I was coming to report Oyamo the Luo. This shamba manager was called "Murungaru". That means straight like a club. Mr. Deakson was his main name. He said approach the main office.

Before I reached I met with Mrs. Karen, and Mr. Thomas, and Mr. Barance Blixen. I greeted them and they replied kindly. Mrs. Karen asked whether I knew the names of the dogs they had with them. I told her yes: One was panya, one Dusk, and the last one was Askari. When she heard this she was much delighted. She told me, "Oh thanks."

PANIA,

DUSK,

ROUGE.

She told me to draw near as to give me a sweet. I was afraid of the horse she went on, so she told me not to fear. I took sweets and granted her thanks. Where I was going? I told her that I was heading to the office to accuse one Luo who ran away with my money of a hen (the amount of six shillings). She looked into my basket and found the roots of trees as my medicine. Kindly she told me to follow her up to her house. But I was fearing the dogs. She told me to fear not. Dusk was the worst of all the two ones. He was later to cause deaths.

So Mrs. Karen, after reaching home, told the cook Isa, Akamba in tribe, to boil water in a kettle as to wash my leg. She went first to the other shamba, upper one, to where that Luo worked to settle matters.

The cook was to put the boiled water into a debbe and the water mixed with medicine. Then put my leg into that water untill she came back from home of the main manager who abused me by kicking and by hand. I stayed in water untill half past five. She then

rentered the house and washed me very kindly. That leg was to be washed until red germs was seen. The whole wound was covered with liquid diseased yellow. I was tied up with medicine, and was told to come the following day. I thanked her and went.

After reaching, my mother asked me where did you go? And what is that on your leg? I told her that I was tied up by Mrs. Karen. They got worried that I might make them be expelled from the shamba. I asked her whether she wanted me to die, or what? My mother asked me, if we are charged for your treatment where are we going to get money? I told her that I never told Mrs. Karen to treat me, she treated me for her own mercy.

When it was day, I started leaping onward to Karen House. Mrs. Karen saw me and said so you have come? They had not yet taken their breakfast. She told her cook to do the same thing of boiling water. After that Mrs. Karen washed my leg and I was tied boiling. Then she asked her cook whether there was food in the store.

KAREN HOUSE 1922

"I had a farm in Africa, at the foot of the Ngong Hills . . . it was Africa
distilled up through six thousand feet, like the strong and refined essence of a continent."

"The merriment ran along the terrace and spread to the edge of it like ripples on water.
There are few things in life as sweet as this suddenly rising, clear tide of African laughter."

He said that there was sugar in a bag, rice
in the corner and even unga (flour).   He was told to
give me two pounds from every portion and to
go home.   Mrs. Karen told me to turn back
and tell my mother to be cooking for me
because I was quite unhealthy.   I was
given my loads and also one shoe for the
good foot.   I worried how I would travel with
one shoe and a stake, but I leaped as
far as my home.

my medicines

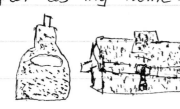

Kg

When my mother saw me with the food she was
about to beat me.   Who told you to go and get
foods, when we have that here?   Who will
pay for that?   My mother rebuked me and
then she got the rice and potatoes.   She
made porride with a little sugar, and I
took it.   I went on going to Mrs. Karen
but the leg never got quite better. Mrs.
Karen told that now his leg of Kamande was
deteriable.   This leg has defeated me.
  Every day it uses a bottle of medicine.
What you will do is to stay with me in my

house and I try to treat you... Well,
I went and belonged and then she was
going to take me to Kikuyu Hospital. Her
treatment was unsuceeding. She told Farah
and Juma that they were going to Nairobi
to get food and clothing. Mrs. Karen
bought two red blankets and two sheets.
Now you are going to Scotland Mission Hospital,
Kikuyu, and the place might be very cold during
nights so get these blankets and be covering

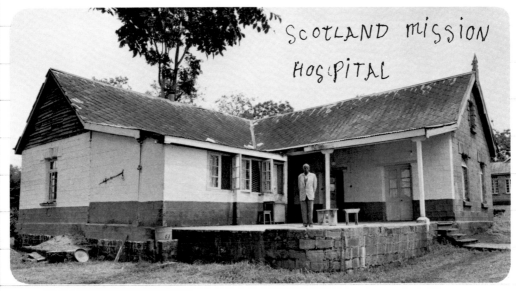

SCOTLAND MISSION
HOSPITAL

SAMSON AND MRS NJOROGE

yourself with them.   The top Doctor
Arthur will look after this Leg in the
hospital.   She called for my younger
brother, Titi, who was even bigger than
me for he had not suffered any disease.
He was to carry these blankets up to the
hospital with me we went on foot for there
weren't a car to help us.   At nightfall,
we were to sleep in a place which was
near Dagoretti.

   Now my leg was hurting. In the
Scotland Mission hospital we gave people
the lettler from Mrs. Karen.   It had
eighty shillings inside.   We had been
warned not to give the lettler to anybody
else apart from the doctor in charge.
I gave it to the head dresser who was
known as Samson Njoroge.   After that
the doctor in charge called Dr. Arthur,
read the same news, and he order for
2 more blankets and searched me a good
bed made with a zebra skin and cloths.

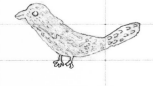

I was well covered with blankets and the two I brought with me.

In the following day I was put under the medicine which smelt very disagreeably. I stayed with it but the leg never improved. I called for Samson and told him " This leg of mine is not curing. Just look where the bandages tie is still with skuds." When the doctor came he saw that my disease was serious and one of my hands was very unable to handle anything.

This Leg was taking me away. Samson
said that the disease would be Looked
after in best manner and if it defeated
them they would set me free to go to
my homes and die there. The foLLowing
day they were to take me to the mortuary
for operation. It was managed by Daniel
Kabucho Who could touch bodies. I was
told not to eat anything by evening. I was
done the operation. I reaLLy ran mad
because I never realised anybody around
me the Whole time. I was taken back
to my bed, and When I woke up, started
singing madLy.

Nyani na ndege

Kamante

Karen Langata

I was told by those doctors to sleep.
They proposed to inject me to see
whether I would improve. Each
injection cost Mrs. Karen 40/= and she
paid 80/= for two.

My illness improved slowly and slowly
I untied my leg and my hurting hand was
then a bit better. I sat one day near
the kitchen and could look away to Kikuyu
station. In my heart it looks like Mrs.
Karen coming to the hospital. She made
a halt just by the junction to Kikuyu and
to the hospital. I woke up and went to
her with Samson the dresser and we shook
hands happily.

Mrs. Karen told me to turn on the
coming Thursday exactly at 10 o'clock...
As to make her sure whether I was
all right. I told her all right if I'm
permitting. I ran to the road to wave
goodbye. We parted and she went onward.

On the following Thursday, I asked for
permission to go home for greetings and was
allowed. After reaching I was shown a very
good house just within Mrs. Karen's home.

My duty would be to oversee little boys
that were cooking for her dogs. My
duty would be to see the dogs eating
satisfactorily. I untied myself to
her joy.

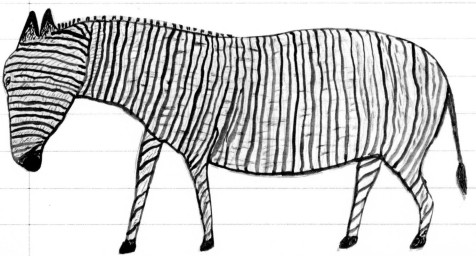

Karen Blixen and her friend Ingrid Lindstrom

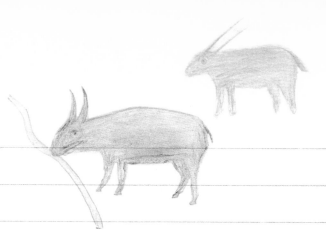

"A bald, skinny bird of prey of a
dying species"

"Dignified, gentle ways . . .
with a laughter like silver bells"

Mrs. Karen with (left to right) Farah, his son Saufe, Ali Hassan, and Tumbo, son of Juma

THE GOODNESS OF MRS. KAREN
CHAPTER 3

Coffee harvest … Mrs. Karen much liked …
one cow for each tribe … Hassan Ismael,
Farah Aden, and the other Somali,
Ali Juma

Bror Blixen inspecting cultivation

The place was very much delt with in cultivation

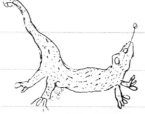

PANIA ISAJ DUSK

"I was filled with admiration for my coffee-plantation, that lay quite bright green in the grey-green land."

CHAPTER 3

THE GOODNESS OF MRS. KAREN

Mrs. Baroness was very fond of Looking toward the Ngong Hills. From her home and even from my grandmother's hut sitting on a native stool she did Look From my grandmother's hut, the sight of Ngong was clear and no thickets prevented her from observing.

Karen of nowadays was Karen coffee then. When the farm was new, many people were employed for cutting trees. After cutting there were groups of people for cultivating. Then after it was cultivated there was planted beans. The place was very much delt with in cultivation untill it was fine enough for coffee. There was such great rainfall that the coffee grew and brought harvests. Mrs. Barance Karen, we called her "Mama" She thought of going to England for a machine. The machine just came. There was one Indian responsible for it known as Bulsingh and the manager of the farm was known as Deakson. He had another undermanager called "Makanyanga"

meaning "heavy Walking." The coffee became so much that no other thing brought
as much wark as coffee Karen of nowadays
was Karen coffee farm then — Therefor
the garden was bigger for, coffee than for
others. There was three wagons brought
for carrying harvest to Nairobi. Two
wagons were having thirty two bulls,
meaning 16 apiece, and the third one was
small with eight bulls. Also in these
wagons were two drivers and one Kikuyu,
Mushika—Kamba,

guiding. The drivers

of the wagons had to
walk. When we had
to take coffee to
Nairobi, we were
Leaving at 2 p.m

Oxen pulling a coffee wagon

and we used to
sleep at Kiria Nugu,
now named colonial
store. Next dawn
proceding Nairobi we
had to Leave coffee
in the railway store.

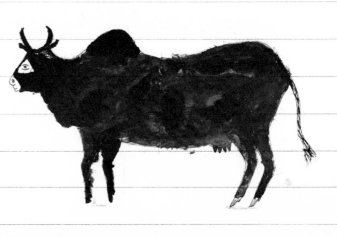

Mrs. Karen finally had a motor car with a Somali driving called Farah Aden by name, and if she wanted to go to Nairobi, she had to be driven in it

Kamante

Karen Blixen was so much liked by all people in Karen. For she was kind to anybody who was working on other farms.

That means if somebody was chased away by his master she would employ him in her garden and give him places to build his house, together with a piece of land where he could grow some crops.

Many people proceded from Majeng, Ruiru, Thika, Nairobi, even from Uganda and from Mombasa to stay. She would not expel those who were staying in her farm without working. She only liked them. In actual fact she employed a lot of Moslems.

She was indeed and axcellent woman, because she never hated anybody or doctrine, even Mohammedans.

Every Tuesday and Thursday Mrs. Karen was very glad to give me tobbacco

and young men each a packet
of ciggarrets, known as Kingstork,
and the children were getting sugar and
coins such as five cents to make them
happy. The goodness of the shamba
was that we could'nt suffer from lack
of food, and every Fraiday Mrs. Karen
used to slaughter five cattle for
her workmen. When the animals were
divided among the people, each animal
spared either a leg or a hand for the dogs.
     The meat was always shared
into tribes because there were many
different ones working there. She divided
those cows: Wakamba one cow,

"The discovery of the dark races was to me
a magnificent enlargement of all my world."

DUSH

"A link between the life of my civilized house and . . . the wild"

MRS. KAREN

the manager Deakson's Home

Meru one cow, Embu one cow, and some others working there got one cow also. I myself used to give persons three pounds meat. The person who was slaughtering was known as Hassan Ismael, an Islam. This was his buisness. The Somalis also had a whole village in Karen Garden but I could not understand their language. We found that they don't like each other while eating as they were not eating together.

There was once a quarrel between Hassan Ismael and Farah Aden who was overseer at Karen. I never knew why those troubles occured but the family of Ismael had come with guns to kill Farah Aden. Farah was helped by another Somali known as Ali Juma. When Mrs. Karen heard this, she was very annoyed and carried Juma and them to Nairobi for a trial in front of Somalil master. No death occured. And each of them was given a shop (the Karen stores of nowadays).

On the front lawn

WA-KIKUYUS 1921

"A stage of the first order, it collected all the colours and movements . . . into a unity."

In reality Mrs. Barance was all good because even police could'nt enter into her shamba to trouble people. She used to tell them _her_ _shamba_ is hers and she knows how to regulate her people. She would'nt prevent us from keeping cows or sheep in our camps. So nobody took the shamba to be of Europeans. We took it to be ours. We found this garden belonging to all of us. Therefore we had no idea of leaving the garden... She told her peoples that everybody came from God and even lions. She was really Godly and peacefull. Everybody wanted to stay there until deaths of them all.

POLICE

Therefore we found this woman was kind and merciful to everybody at Ngong. If we speak the truth this woman was with God and that is most simply true because she was saying that not even a bird or this garden is mine. ALL belongs to God. As it was hard circumstances that made her leave Karen, everybody working in her farm felt very bad because their aim was to stay fore ever.

Mrs. Karen

MRS. KAREN'S FIRST CAR

"People work much in order to secure the future;
I gave my mind much work and trouble, trying to secure the past."

my stove
For bathswater

I am fit to rest in kitchen …
the Sultans Cake Book …
Europeans come for my cookery…
my mother dies

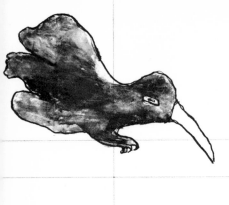

MYSELF KAmante

ISA

ABDULHI

HASSAN ISMAEL

Juma and mahu

tumbo

ALI HASSAN

Mrs. Karen Liked panya
very much because it
was not cruel as Askari
and Dusk

CHAPTER 4

OF MY COOKERY AND SOME TROUBLES

One day Mrs. Karen told me that we should start Learning Education. Shamba people were reading Education during the night and we did read also during the day after Lunch. I was told to go and get books from the Scotland Mission at Kikuyu. I was not going back to my mother, Since I was to stay with Mrs. Karen and enjoy Karen School.

The whole time I stayed until one Mkamba boy called Esa worked cooking in the kitchen found himself poisoned and he became murdered. Then Mrs. Karen told me to go to the kitchen helping Hassan Ismael in washing utensils. I had been working in both places, Looking after dog cook as well as serving the kitchen cleaning. Now I could wash Sufferias and dust out the ovens. Hassan said I was fit to rest by him in the kitchen because everything was sudden tidy. He told me that Gitau, the other boy,

never dusted the cookers or swept away
the floor. He was only resting idle. Mrs. Karen
came every day and said my service was
excellent. From then I had to rest
in the Kitchen instead. I assisted Hassan
until I was able to bring on some cakes
and food.

Mrs. Karen taught me very much
about cookery and couldn't mind even
when Hassan went to Nairobi. She was
teaching me with a book known as the
Sultan cake Book. It is a thick book
containing all sorts of styles of cooking.
I was wanting to be a cook but due to
childhood difficulties I refused. At last
I realized how Mrs. Karen helped me and
my hands from a fatal illness and I agreed.
Esa Farthall was completely murdered
by that disease of poisoning and I henseforth
was cooker.

If there came visitors, she had
to send me to the Library for the Sultan
Book of Cookery ; She could read to
us the sort of food we had to make. She
could even tell me to go and search for
some wild vegetables which we Kikuyu

KAREN DUKAS

Liked very much, known as _terere_. I put
toasts inside, they really left the food
sweet and nourishing. I tried sweet
potatoes and also put one into every egg
and still that was very sweet food for
her. I then could get maize and put them
into pieces, mix with milk and wetflour
and after that put it into an oven that
made almost a Queens cake.

Many Europeans came us to see my
cookery. I had to cook a fish with egg
at the top and no bones. Such could
make them very much happy. Once,
there came very important people:
Prince of Wales and Duke of Wales.
I had to cook avery strange fish got from
Mombasa; it is the crab one with many
legs and arms. I had to boil it so as

at Karen Farm

to take off the skin; then take off its
meat and mix with a sauce and salad.
I even cooked ducks and turkeys. I had
to cook a lot of food differently, especially
when those two kings children had come
for visit.

I stayed cooking until my mother got
burnt. She was carried to the hopital
with a sack and she gloriously died.
She left three children and with me
four. Three were men and one girl.
I was very much worried with the death of
mama for there was a very young
baby she left. The baby was
six months and I had no cows.
I had troubles. I told my
younger brother who was abit
sensible to take the baby
to my grandmother. I never
wanted anything like money ... What I wanted
was only food to help my mother's children.
Our salary by then was four shillings
per month. Mrs. Karen told me to go to
Bul singh who was the manager of the machine
and that whenever my grandmother came

to him she should carry away anything she
liked. The Indian -- (after giving him the
letter) -- asked me how he would recognise
my grandmother among other women to give
her food. I told him that I would be
coming with her to make him know her.
She was given three debbies of maize fat for
cooking for the children. The children were
Titi and Watiri. I was also given sugar to
take home. I really thanked God for giving
me such help from Mrs. Karen for those children
never died from starving. Really, had it
not been for my thoughts of going to accuse
the Luo, we never would have met with truthful

THE POND   Mrs Karen

Mrs. Karen. God and Mrs. Karen helped the children
from dying. My father had died in the shamba and
my mother too. I couldn't blame anybody and only
the Mighty new reasons of these two deaths.

THE NGONG FOREST

CHAPTER 5

Buffalo, leopards, and no elephants...
forest hunts... lions inside Lendela's boma...
Kandisi Hill

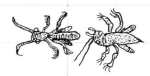

MR. BLIXEN

CHAPTER 5

THE NGONG FOREST

Mrs. Karen had given us some plots for cultivating and you could plant anything that pleased you. The crops were doing well. Everybody wanted to stay in the garden until ever and ever. In that Ngong farm there were also buffalos, Leopards and no elephants, but Sometimes Hipopotomas were coming. Monkey were there always. Before the farm was ploughed out many animals were coming from many places; futhermore Mrs. Karen Blixen was a hunter. She was often collecting some people to go to the forest to hunt the animals. Therefore that forest was once full of animals but all ran away to far places except some of the buffalos and leopards. Gatura forest was nearby and animals fled for there. ("Gatura" is a small squirrel) But in that forest were soon very many people. They therefore were making big fires in different places so the animals could went away. It was like that.

Mr. Barance Blixen, the husband of Mrs. Karen, was also hunter. He used to call for people and go in the shamba to drive away the animals.

He would tell people not to make noise. He could shoot bullets to them until they went on the other side of MasaiLand.

Farah also did play with a bow and arrow but he never knew how to set it. He could pull the string and yet not the arrow and it fell on his foot. I used to Laugh telling him that arrows and bows are from Wakamba. He better could joke with

"It may be said that hunting is ever a love-affair. The hunter is in love
with the game, real hunters are true animal lovers."

a pistol because he had expersence there.

Ostriches were so many in the shamba
because they Like some plantation place
with high grass.   The ostriches used to
go to another farm Which we called Gatura
Farm where now are houses of cripples
and handless people.

ALL animals got Lost from the farm
because people had built houses 'everyWhere
with cattle and they were holding night dances
of old men, Women and young men, and the noise

was great.

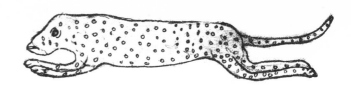

One day one Lion went inside the cattle _boma_
of LendeLa the masai chieftain. Lendela's
farm was nearby ours of Mrs. Karen for many
Masai built their manyatta near Langata.
Mrs. Karen used to walk through the masai
farm with her horses.

Next door in Angata Rongai too there
is a place where she was always going, up
to _Kandisi HiLL_, Sometimes Known as
Lions hill. She could see far, She
thought to be burried on Lions hiLL.

"Long perspectives stretch before me, distance is the password of the scenery;
at times I feel that the fourth dimension is within reach. I fly, in dream, to any altitude,
I dive into bottomless, clear, bottle-green waters."

Mr. Blixen, two cattle-killers, and, on the right, Farah

MR BARANCE BLIXEN   FARAH

ME AND LULU
CHAPTER 6

Mrs. Karen finds the bush buck baby…
I am its parent … Lulu has preginance …
the friend stays in forest … her bell is lost

KAMANTE GATURA
KAREN LANGATA

"Her ears were smooth as silk and exceedingly expressive.
Her nose was as black as a truffle.
Her diminutive hoofs gave her all the air of a young Chinese lady . . . with laced feet.
It was a rare experience to hold such a perfect thing in your hands."

CHAPTER 6
ME AND LULU

Mrs. Karen was a joyous woman. One day on her way to Nairobi, she stopped for children.

They did shield a young bush buck! She gave them warnings to guard it for her returning. She had said that she was to eat at Norfolk Hotel for lunch so we all knew that no food was to be cooked during lunch. At four o'clock she came and parked the car by the store. She told me there that she had to come with LuLu. I looked. It was a bush buck baby. She asked me how I was going to look after it. It was only done to be giving it some milk. I was told to care for it very much.

Kinuthia asked me, "Where shall we keep it as not to be lost?" I said in the visitors' bath room because it was not used. After cooking my food, I used to take sacks and make a place for LuLu to sleep on. In the morning, LuLu was opened by me and given warm milk. It learned to suck

Like a baby. I was told to treat it like
a motherless calf so I had to give it
a bottle like a human baby. I would
search for a soda bottle and warm the
milk. If she got not satisfied with one
bottle, I added more milk. I tamed it
very much until it came to know that I
was its parent. It was accustomed with
house and dogs and they could all of
them follow me when I was on a bicycle,
even to Nairobi.

I told Mrs. Karen to give me money
so as to buy LuLu a bell. The bell
was to tie round LuLu's neck as to be
ringing where ever she walked. I went to
Dagoretti and bought two bells each one
shilling. I tied LuLu the bell and she
was very happy. She joked with the bell
on the grass ringing now and then.

LuLu grew very big and stopped to
suck milk. She was eating grass and
some leaves, even sometimes potatoe vines
and salt. If she went to the forest
and I call for her with fond voice, she
came quickly because she was knowing

that I was calling for sugar and salt reasons. She liked me very much particularly.

Then I noticed that _LuLu_ hadpreginance. I told Mrs. Karen and was refused because she said _LuLu_ had not that time to go out. Mrs. Karen told me that if she did meet _LuLu_ with a baby, after staying for six months in Europe, she would give me a calf. After she went _LuLu_ gave birth to a baby female.

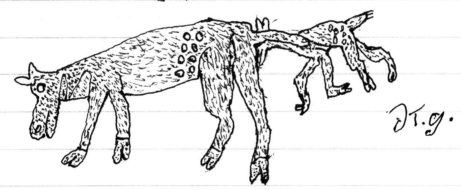

I went to the manager and told him that LuLu gave birth. He came quickly after finishing with stores. After he found that it was true he was very happy. He said that he would send an information to Mrs. Karen in Europe. Mrs. Karen received the news and was very gay. She came after holidays and met _LuLu_ with a baby.

THE COLLAR AND BELLS THAT I MADE *K.g.*

K.g.

"Lulu came to my house from the woods as Kamante had come to it from the plains."

One day she told me to call because
LuLu was away from home.   When she
heard my voice, LuLu came running
from the forest accompained by a buck.
Mrs. Karen thus knew the origin of the womb.

We stayed with LuLu and she had
another womb.   She gave birth to
another baby famale.   Then she had
two young ones female.   After some
months she had yet another, a baby male.
There were four bucks including the
babies' mother LuLu.   LuLu's friend
would not come straight to the people.
It would be left a far by LuLu When
I called.   LuLu's children feared me
but not very much.   They could run
away but not far.

I could get hold of only her firstborn. We stayed for avery long time. Her man friend was coming from the forest at night and after seeing the people ran back away to the forest. But Lulu would not run away and her children all were left on the grass playing. When the night drew near Lulu slept by the road with her children without any fear of people at all.

The firstborn of Lulu gave birth and we stayed for four days without knowing that there was a baby born. When we knew, we went and that child was fearing us. It had not seen people before.

I called for Lulu once and found that she had no bell. I don't know who had cut it. She came as usual and licked sugar and salt, but her children could not came near. After finishing, she went and drunk on the verander.

When Mrs. Karen went away, I left Lulu and the six young ones still in that forest near Karen House. After we shifted, I can't tell clearly when Lulu died because she and her family were never hunted. (End.)

Thieving in the home…the <u>Muganga</u> comes…
a small boy with money…
Mrs. Karen takes care

FARAH ADEN

CHAPTER 7

A MATTER OF JUSTICE

Police never came at Mrs. Karen's. Only
one day Farah Aden said that there was
a thieving in the home. Police asked how
many people wanted to leave their job
because then they steal when hoping to
depart. We were asked for how long we
had stayed on the job. Farah said he
instead would find it all out and he called
for a witchdoctor as to know exactly
who had stolen that money. The Muganga
is he who can tell the truth through any
wall. The Muganga who was called Ngala
elected to provide all those peoples in the
garden with a bread, and if somebody who
had took the money ate it he die. When
people heard, they were asking that Muganga
give them bread.

During the police
inquired about our services...
I said I had stayed there for
fifteen years. Farah was
not asked because he was
the overseer of the house.

Mrs. Karen told the police to go, she will
investigate the money by herself with Farah.
Police told us that if we fail to say out
loud who had the money, they will imprison
him for ten years in jail.

It came to be known that a small
boy was the victim. It was as follows:
This boy was to go and carry meat from
Karen stores. Juma gave the boy
one extra shilling to buy some cigarettes.

The boy thought he got a chance to change
his stolen money into shillings. He took
his 20 shilling note, then gave out the note
to Nuru of the Karen store. Nuru had
heard of the thefte. He wondered where
the boy got such money. So he told the
boy, " Who gave you this amount?" The
boy answered that he was given it by Juma,
a note of five schillings he said. The boy
was given cigarettes, but Nuru did not refund
the change to the boy. The boy carried
the cigarettes to Juma and a letter from
Nuru. In it was written, " Search the
money from that boy... He produced
a 20/= note and said it was a five shilling;

NYORE

MASAILAND DUKA

Kg

He doesn't know money."

__ALi Muchaga__ found the boy shaking.

ALi Muchaga was the person who used to go for safaris with a European known as Mr. pinjo-Hatern. When the boy found that he will be known, he returned the money into the store where I was keeping things for cooking. The young boy who was known as __Nyore Kiingu__, was almost leaving his "__Karen coffee__" job to go to his father in the __Rift valley__. The boy had found where Farah kept the keys of the safe, so he took the keys and stole three hundread and sixty shillings. That boy was liked by Mrs. Karen very much. She used to send the boy to go to see is anybody fishing from the pond nearby.

__ALi Muchaga__ spied the boy in that store and wondered exactly why he was there as there wasn't anything concerning him. The boy became nervous and truly started shivering. Farah Aden was suspecting grown-up people.

ALi Muchaga told everybody that the money has been stolen by the little boy __Nyore__. Everybody wondered.

Nuru the shop keeper asked the boy, "young boy, how much did you give me?" The boy said that he gave <u>Nuru five shilling note</u>. And where was the rest of the money? The boy crazily said that he had bought meat with some other boys and eate it in the forest. He was told not to be mad, all lost money is with <u>Msabu Blixen</u>.

He was then a bit beaten but not very much because Mrs. Karen refused. Msabu said this is a little boy who never knew what he, was doing. Because the boy was to go with his father shortly in the Rift valley, she had planned to give him 200 shillings for the very good service of looking after the pond that it was not being fished. This now could be less.

The pond, "always much alive, with a ring of cattle and children round it"

Plucking coffee ... many tribes ...
a fall from the wagon ... dog fear brings death ...
we dig a pit

WāmBui
Kanandl

WāmBu.
Ka Hoi

nduta
Kuriz

CHAPTER 8

WAMBUI KAHOI MEETS DEATH

During our work in the coffee plantation, the day was filled after plucking three debbies, and if we were able to pluck more than three we had to be paid the rest over.

Once the machine for washing caught fire and a bag of coffee roasted. There wasn't a very great destruction of the machine, it was only necessare to repair the places destroyed. It was working day and night. There were people of the day and people of the night.

When all was ready sorted beans were packed on the wagons to be taken to Nairobi. The journeys were a bit tremendous because there were not as good roads as there are today. The roads were poor because of passing herds of cattle, wagons and rain. On the way back from Nairobi coffee stores, the bulls would crawl tiredly.

The coffee factory "hung in the great African night like a bright jewel in an Ethiope's ear."

After reaching home they used to be freed from the wagons and stay for three days without working.

Mrs. Karen had to tell her people not to have quarrels and if anybody quarreled she got very angry. She used to tell everybody that if they bring quarrels they were going to prevent <u>rain</u> from falling on the shamba. She was praying God to bring peace and compromise into her <u>shamba</u>. She never wanted any tribalism: <u>MKamba</u>, <u>Meru</u>, <u>Masai</u>,

coffee factory

Somali or Kikuyu. "I want
you to be good people of God";
We all agreed with her.

Every tribe had their own overseer
or Msimamizi. Wakamba with their,
Kikuyu as well, and even Merus
the same. For Kikuyus he is the
Nyabara. It came to pass that the
upper Kenton shamba had a lot of coffee.
Young men and women were told to go and
pluck it. Going back home, there
were three girls and they were known
as Njeri Njuguna, Wambui Njuguna and
Wambui Kahoi, who met misfortune.

They said that they were to ride
on the wagon which carried the coffee
they had plucked. As the wagon was
very heavy, it was pulled by a lot of oxen.
They were about Karen House when they
were to alight as not to be eaten by
" Dusk, "othe crueler dog of Mrs. Karen.
They had to jump from the wagon when
going.

Wambui Kahoi jumped and her
basket clinged on the wagon. The
driver knew nothing and the girl fell

and the wagon passed over her chest.
She died and the others cried out and
the dogs ran to their sides.

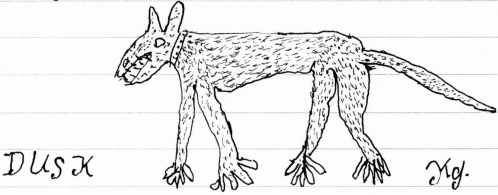

DUSK   Kg.

When Mrs. Karen heard this she went
rushing and told the parents, your daughter
is dead through bad fortune and you should
come.   They refused and said that
they had not to go and see a corpse.
Mrs. Karen came and told me, "Kamande,
your tribe is very tough because even
parents refuse to see their own daughter
in death." She really spoke kindly and
said that if they came she could help
them with nine hundred shillings because
it was not her fault or the girl's fault,
only dog fear that brought the danger.
Afterwards she sent some soldiers to
go and call the girl's parents.   Kahoi
the father refused to see them and his

wife and brother refused. During the nighttime Mrs. Karen called for me and asked me what we had to do. I told her that she only had to send for three people to dig the hole for the girl. It was bad because the girl had stayed five days on the very spot she was killed. Then Mrs. Karen called for three people, Merus by tribe, and told them they should be taking care of the dead girl.

The pit was ready, six feet deep, and after they finished they sent one person for us. But we meet nobody... The Merus, they all three had escaped from the grave in fear.

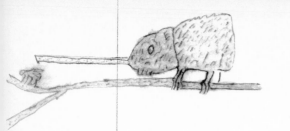

Mrs. Karen told me to hold Wambui Kahoi
by the head and she had to hold her
by the food and we carried her exactly
to the pit.   In death she
had everything with her, even the basket
and her clothes and necklaces.   But we
were very angry with those parents for
loosing their daughter thus.   We carried
her to the pit and let her plunge.   We had
no shovels to throw soil.   So we used our
hands.   It was such a wark that Mrs.
Karen told us to be leaving it and she
went to Mr. Deackson asking where the
three Merus had come.   She told the
three Merus to turn.   Then we told them
to put themselves the soil back into the
pit so they agreed with us.

        The parents of the dead girl
escaped to the Rift valley with the
whole family.   The brother of Kahoi,
known as Kega, was abandoned behind.
Mrs. Karen asked him why did your father
fail to bury his daughter? ... Mrs. Karen
was ready to help them if they agreed.

Now, she said, to whom am I going to
help about the dead girl?

That is how I found one mistake in the
behavior of the Karen workers. I never
wondered so much of the mother of the
girl; but of the father Kahoi and of
his son failing to bury their daughter
I felt very bad.

Mrs. Karen told us we should not fear
death because everybody is awaited by death.

On Karen Road where Wambui Kahoi met death

THE VOICE OF THE GUN

CHAPTER 9

Kitchen jokes … houseboy shoots …
a night drive to Nairobi hospital …
Wanyangii is sewed up … case of the dead Muturi

"The . . . old men sat around, infinitely attentive, and with all their wits collected for the proceedings."

CHAPTER 9

THE VOICE OF THE GUN

One night we heard the voice of the gun.
Mrs. Karen asked me where the gun shot
was. I told her that it had cracked
just near the coffee machine. She ordered
for Farah to start the car. Before we set
off, we heard the motor cycle of Mr.
Makanyanga, called Mr. Bellnap, charging.
We waited for him quickly. He was asked
what's wrong; he had been eating and he
heard a noise of a gun in the kitchen.
Even he hadn't finished eating. The matter
was as follows:

There had come some boys to visit at
Karen. Then when the food was at the
fire they started joking. The house boy
told them he knew how to shoot yet he
never knew whether the gun had bullets.
He pulled the trigger and found both
bullets. There was a very great
explosion hitting the pans. The pans
were hard and turned the bullets to the
boys. The bullets met Muturi and
Wanyangii. They cut Muturi by the chest

and Wanyangii was cut in his Lower jaw.

We met them each Lying far from the other one. Wanyangii was saying OOOOO! OOOOO! and Muturi was saying grmmmmm! with death pains. There was Laid sacks in the car and we carried them to the hospital of K.A.R. I was between them holding them lightly. Muturi was so very uncontious that he was strightening his Legs infront and pushed Mrs. Karen and Farah to the ceiling. I Kept on holding them up to the Hospital. Before taking them in, Muturi died. Wanyangii was Left alive with his jaw one half off.

He was Left in the hospital and we went to Nairobi. We went into very many offices

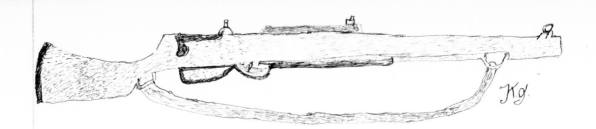

where I could not know what Mrs. Karen
was saying.   Then we returned home.
Wanyangii was treated until his tongue was
returned inside his mouth because it was
outside before.   He was sewed until goodness.
He stayed for four months in the hospital,
and we were taking food and oranges
to him.   After that he was set free.

Then he came home.   He had to be
helped. At Karen shamba there was soon
a case of the dead Muturi.   His parents
Njuguna and Kaninu wanted to claim for his
person. Chief Kinyanjui was called by Mrs. Karen.
He was told by her to judge traditionally
about the dead boy for if the   shooter,
Kabiru by name, was taken to the government,
he could be hanged.   Muturi who died was
to be paid 50 goats, which is 1,000/,—,
and Wanyangii who was alive was paid 600/—
for his taken-out teeth.

Kabiru was only a small boy and was
joking. He never knew what he was doing.
The case was settled by the Wazees and
the case got signed and was no more quarrels
had.   Kabiru by then had long escaped
over to MasaiLand.

On the plain:
"As if it were all the stars of heaven
running wild over the sky"

He hide in Masailand for a long while. He was fearing otherwise he could be killed by government. But when Mrs. Karen went to Europe, he was seen walking disguised with the Masai at Ngong. He was told not to fear for every case against him was finished; but ever he returned to Masailand.

Sometime after he got married and the wife died ... Then he married another one and she died. At last he went to Arusha alone to cultivate a shamba. Even now he is down there by Tanganyika. If you see Kabiru walking you would think he was a Masai warrior, for he walks exactly Masai.

We had all thought that he, Kabiru, never knew about guns; but if he had killed with a spear, that would be another case.

"To the West, the Hills before us, with a little floating
grey mist in the creeks, lived gravely through
another moment of their many thousand years. . . .
As night fell, the four peaks seemed to be flattened
and smoothened out, as if the mountain was
stretching and spreading itself."

"A lion on the plain bears a greater likeness to ancient monumental stone lions than to the lion which to-day you see in a zoo; the sight of him goes straight to the heart."

"We put down domestic animals as respectable and
wild animals as decent, and held that [the latter] stood
in direct contact with God. . . .

"Must there then, even in Africa, be no live creature
standing in direct contact with God?"

"Looking back on my life in Africa,
I feel that it might altogether be described
as the existence of a person
who had come from a rushed and noisy world,
into a still country."

". . . . country so lovely, as if the contemplation
of it could in itself be enough
to make you happy all your life."

"In very old days the elephant, upon the roof of the earth, led an existence deeply satisfying to himself and fit to be set up as an example to the rest of creation."

". . . the mighty peaceful beasts . . . their long horns streaming backwards over their raised necks, the large loose flaps of breastskin, that make them look square, swaying as they jog. They seem to have come out of an old Egyptian epitaph."

"Serious-minded, self-sufficient neighbours,
the old nobility of the hills"

"I had seen a herd of Buffalo . . .
come out of the morning mist under a copper sky, one by one,
as if the dark and massive, iron-like animals . . .
were being created before my eyes and sent out as they were finished."

"...they came out of the woods and went back again as if my grounds were a province of the wild country."

The hundred children of Kinanjui …
dancing for the chief … asleep in drink …
a swollen leg … we go to his funeral

"Kinanjui . . . stared straight in front of him in order that I should see his
face in profile like a head struck upon a medal."

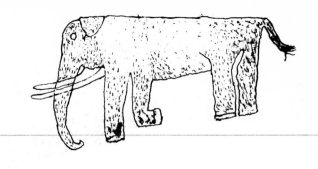

CHAPTER IO

PARAMOUNT CHIEF KINYANJUI

Chief Kinyanjui was so rich that he had thirteen wives in MasaiLand and in his home at Kawongware he had thirty wives. The children who were born in MasaiLand got married Later to Masai people. These children were so many that he couldn't know them. Yau could see about hundred children calling one person daddy, for they knew their father.

All chiefs wanted to visit Karen House. When they were to come, Mrs. Karen called the old Mzees Like Ruiyana, Kaninu and Kamiriti for entertainment. Mrs. Karen told people that they had to dance for the chiefs, there was to be rejoicing for Kinyanjui was to visit. He was a good man and could settle any case in the shamba. She could not know what old Kikuyu Wazees Liked for their meat, so I told her that they Liked meat and beer. Then she could send Farah with a car to the Butchery to be bringing meat and breads. Meat also was provided for the dancers. She told me

to make a lot of coffee and mix with beer.
After that she ordered for chairs to be
kept in her husband's office because it was
large enough to fit many people.

The day of the visits was of great joy.
For that chief was liked by Mrs. Karen very
much. He was also of High Rank because
he was paramount chief. I was told to
take every food to chiefs. After the meat
was over and everyone was drinking, the chiefs
would tell Mrs. Karen that they had to go
and would return another day. But once
Kinyanjui found himself, asleep in drink,
stretched along Karen terrace. This
was unlawful and punishable by D.C.
against giving drink. But Kinyanjui soon was
woken away.

Before departing happily to their
homes, the chief and his <u>Wazees</u> always
wished Mrs, Karen intelligence and honour.
Chief could be given a car driven by Farah
for escort.

He once went to his home in Masailand
when his cattle were coming. He was walking
and supervising them when he stepped on

a cut-out small piece of tin and was injured. His leg got swollen very much. At last he was very uncontious and died. We went to his funeral with a car and Mrs. Karen carried a lot of flowers for he used to be such a good friend. Everyone attended this funeral. Kinyanjui had a fine robe he was wearing.

Wounderously enough he had no educated child. Only one used brains from the school at Nairobi and died. It is said that he was poisened by chief Lenana's child who used to say that Kikuyu shouldn't be so rich at Masailand.

Kinyanjui's grave is even now in existance for his sons Daudi and Kigathi made it with photosgraph. Daudi Kinyanjui, after the death of his father, horrified the car he was driving very quickly. Kinyanjui was not driven quickly when he was alive. Daudi changed speed and the whole car became skrap.

Ngoma for the Prince of Wales, 1928

NGOMA FOR THE KING'S CHILDREN:
DUKE OF WALES AND PRINCE OF WALES
CHAPTER II

Night dances by flamelight…
entertaining King's children…a spear incident…
dance for the old people

"The greatest social functions of the farm were the <u>Ngomas</u>,—the big Native dances."

"Eroticism runs through the entire existence of the great wanderers."

"The real performers, the indefatigable young dancers,
brought the glory and luxury of the festivity with them."

CHAPTER II

NGOMA FOR THE KING'S CHILDREN:

Duke OF WALES AND PRINCE OF WALES

Traditional dances were held now and then.
There was the Gichukia, Nguru and even
Muchungwa. The Nguru was danced by young
men only without girls. They had to compete
with the other dancers. ALL people from
chief Kinyanjui had to came to Karen for
competition.

After dancing all night, a dancer
might be given a bull or cow by Mrs. Karen
to eat. There was very much joy. Old
men and women and small children might be
given three cattle to eat and not to think
bad. They shared the meat among themselves.
people from Kawangware had to travel far
and were given warm wishes by Mrs. Karen.

Ngomas were sometimes starting at
10 o'clock. The Gichukia was a daring
dance shared by young men and young girls.
There were native ointments and they smeared
themselves too with die, a redwash dug from
the ground. It was a thrilling dance.
They danced happily and looked young.

There was another night dance well

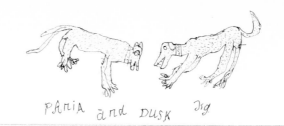

PANIA and DUSK Jg

Known as Mugoiyo young men had to tell girls
to go and look for firewood as the dance
was done deep during night with flamelights
only.   They collected a lot of firewoods
and the dance was first started by men
naked.   Then each girl selected the
boy she liked and stand infront of him
face to face.   For the whole night people
were coming from various places to see
this dance.   Even small boys had their
own dances.

When Duke of Wales and prince
of wales come to visit Mrs. Karen, she
inquired urgently for a night dance from
Kinyanjui's people. Mrs. Karen had ordered
the strong firewoods and had sent girls.
Chief told every young man urgently that
there was a very great dance to be held
at Bogani House (Later Karen) for
entertaining the King's children, Governor
Northinchongo with the two children, and
other important superiors.   The girls
brought a lot of firewoods for that special
dance.   It was started and one Mzee
known as Kibarabara, conductor of the

dance, burnt one person from chief Kinyanjui. Then the brother of that burnt man, known as Kamande Waihumbu, was very angry with the referee. He got his spear and threw it to Kibarabara who was pierced through his bothe Legs. He never minded about the injured Legs only threw his sword to the neck of Kamande Waihumbu.

Mrs. Karen came and told me to go and sleep for I had worked through the day Long.

PRIINCE

AND

DUKE

OF WALES

1928

BY KAMANTE GATURA

"The Son of the Sultan" Edward
Duke of Windsor

I told her that she was to do same herself.
I ran and came with medicine, I tied
Kibarabara and Kamande; then I told
them that I would set them appointment
that day following. I went and finally
slept. There was no more quarrels till
it got finished, they tell me.

Old people were not dancing. Only
one day they had told chief Josiah
that they were to go to Karen House as to
play a dance known only to Wazees
as Muthunguci. Chief refused and said
that such dance is not wanted and people
of his place should not go. Mrs. Karen
sent a letter to D.C. and asked why
old men and women should be refused. She
was told that Josiah had refused it;
Josiah had kept askaris to prevent his
people from going. Then Mrs. Karen
told old people to dance it from her
own shamba without anybody else from
outside. They were shown places
where they could play it and they played.
That was the only dance prevented by
Government.

Then Mrs. Karen had gone to visit England.
When she came back and had not
reached home yet, there was held
a dance of old men known as Muthirigu.
We were told by Deackson that Mrs. Karen
was at Nairobi from Europe and was
coming up presently. We prepared
urgently everything. I knew that she
used to eat at 7:30 p.m. so I made
food and Ali Milo prepared the bed.
We did it quickly so as to ready and
see the dance. That Ngoma for
Mrs. Baraness was sudden. I saw all.

Kikuyu, dazzling in their red chalk coloring:
"The young people themselves look fossilized, like statues cut in rock."

CHAPTER 12
SHORT TALES

General chui

Harry-DAVIDS

1921 — 1925

1921:   Mr. Thomas, Mrs. Karen's
          brother, had a motorcycle
of three wheels called Harrydavids.
After a short period, they bought
a first car. If Mrs. Karen
wanted to go to Nairobi, she
was still going in the motorcycle
with her brother Thomas.
Sometimes the wagon from
Sir Aga Khan with a white
horse had to come with her.
The first car was therefore
in the garage in some pieces.

   1925: Mr. Thomas went to
Europe for he was sent a letter
calling him to go and work
there. The Letter had come
from the King.

THE ANTS MIGHT COME

_or_ Insects Mrs. Karen told us we had to look out for very care fully. Where the ants might come, there was a bitch-dog which was in preginance and if it gives birth, the ants might attack puppies and kill them. So we had to go for inspection within the surrounding forest to see whether there was such trouble - same insects. Whether we found, we poured insectside and pareffin for burning until they all escaped. Mrs. Karen liked her dogs very much.

GOD IS COMING I once saw fire during the night time and I went to call for Mrs. Karen. I told her that Ngong Hill had very great fire. The fire might come from God. She woke from the bed and told me that she would know about it during day time. Ngong Hill is at a distance from Mrs. Karens House so she couldn't go during the night, even if it were God.

DEATH FOR LORD MACMILLAN'S MANAGER

Lord Macmillan was coming to visit Mrs. Karen with his wife. They liked each other. Sometime even they were bringing their dogs because Karen dogs were different from their. They wanted cross breed. He, Macmillan, was so fat that he could not spit infront of his stomach. He could spit sideways. He never entered inside the Karen House. He had to stay on some chair kept on the verandah. He was approximately 400 lbs. Mr. Macmillan's wife was very thin and they used to walk side by side with the Manager of his shamba. We used to say that he Macmillan had no wife. He was so fat that he could have no interest with women. His naming was "Mkora" which is rogue because he had many farms and neved could get settled. He got his small horse under him and went as far as Karen side, from there to Ruiru near Thika and many other places. Macmillan had one shamba near Kikuyu Railway station known as ondiri Farm. Macmillan drowned on his way to Europe after the ship sunk. Macmillan's wife was left on ondiri farm with this Manager when her husband died. They stayed and Mrs. Macmillan gave out a quarry in the farm to a European having not told the manager. The manager was very astonished and he shot himself.

MRS
MACMILLAN

Kg

"MKORA" NA BIBI YAKE

I AM GIVEN A HIT BY HER HAND

One day Mrs. Karen told me that there was to come an old woman visitor. I had to make a cake for the visitor with eggs. Only I said that before she called, I had to go home first. I went knowing that I might not return in time. Soon after I met my people with grass and potato wines. I said that I had to exchange with them quickly and return to the job as to make the cake of the old woman. I had heard Mrs. Karen calling with a loud voice, "Kamande"? I wondered and ran because my house was at a distance. So the visitor had reached long time ago and she had already had coffee taken to her by Juma. Mrs. Karen had struggled to make the cake and she was very angry with me. She asked me, "I told you that there was an old visitor and you went home?" I was given a hit by her hand on my head. I was angry and thought that she was not then giving me respect. I escaped from the house; after a short period, I turned back. That was only the time I cried in her service.

" A SNAKE FROM THE FLOWERS"

There came a snake from the flowers.
The flowers were very closely growing
that only a reptile could hide.   The
snake came and entered Mrs. Karen's
house.   Every person was worried and
started saying what sort of evil is this?
May be devils from the forest.   Mrs. Karen
was angry and asked who has said so?
There is no devil that can come by my home.
Regarderless it was killed and by then I was
far from there for I fear snakes very much.

SNAKES AND BABOONS

One day Askari the dog Son of Mrs. Karen was bitten by a snake. I put medecine and still water was coming from the wound. We took it to the Goan Hospital of dogs just near Norfolk Hotel. It was shaved and bandaged until the wound cured.

Then I walked with the three dogs, DUSK, panya and Askari, Who himself got hold of a Baboon child. The father of the child came and ran to the dog Askari. It was bit by the hand and the rib were broken. It ran to the river and Leaped inside. It did bleed a Lot. I wondered as how I would come to Say Mrs. Karen? Soon she came and asked me, "What"s Wrong with Askari?" I say that they were fighting with an old Baboon for panya had carried their baby. I was told to put it some medicine and tie it.

DUSK

FARAH   MRS KAREN
AND

MR · PINJA - HATERN NEVER FEARED

Mr. Pinja - Hatern, I knew him. One day
addressing me, he said that he had to go for
one year in Somaliland for a hunt of one wild
animal with seven horns on the head. The
animal stays on hills, not on the bottom or
even plains. He went as far as Unjem, staying
for nine months. Then he started his journey
back. He came up to Sagani River. By
then the rain was very heavy and the water
was running over the bridge. He attempted
the car across water. They were swept
with all their belongings. Mr. Pinja-Hatern
was caught by some crocodile on the leg.
Kinuthia and Sharif. He asked them "Are
you approching banks?" They said "yes"
and the first person to get there
was Kinuthia. Sharif came after. Then
the brave European took out his
pocket knife and separated both jaws
of the crocodile. Everything had gone with
the water apart from the clothes they had
worn. They started their journey on foot upto

an Indian <u>Duka</u>.   They called him to open
for it was night.   They asked for blanket
and some shirts to wear during night.
They want to Maragwa and resided in
a hotel, never minding for the drowned car.
He rang to Nairobi for a car and they
were carried again on their journey.

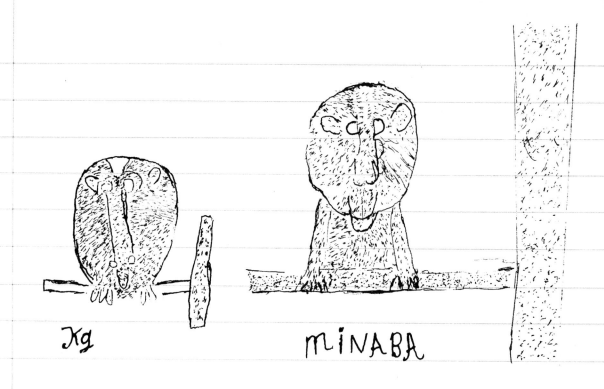

Kg   MINABA

"MINABA" ... IT HAD EARS LIKE A CHILD

Before Mrs. Karen went to Europe she had caught a strang bird, the Gitigi, and she could call it Minaba. That is a kikuyu word for "it had ears Like a child".
The bird Looked Like a person by the face and produced a voice Like a person. The voice said "WO, WO, WO". It was kept in the office of Mr. Blixen who was gone. It was eating 1½ lbs of meat within two days and its drink was milk. I became tame not fearing people. I could carry it on my shoulder and Mrs. Barance also could keep it on the table.

One day the bird was freed from being tied. There was meat on a plate

and the string was still round its leg.
It started playing with the string and
eating the meat. There was nobody in the
house. It swallowed the meat and also
the whole length of string. The whole
string was in its stomach. The bird was
very big and fat. It had learned no
fear with people but it died with the
string

KING STORK
IN KAREN HOUSE

She later got a child of another bird
called Kingstork. The bird was depending
on frogs. There was a system that if a child
brought a gallon of frogs he or she had to
get 50c. That was the job of small boys.
This bird with glittering feathers was very
much beautiful and Mrs. Karen's
favored sight in the Karen house.
It was very good for it never
liked to lead the social
lives with other Kingstorks.
It only played round the house all
alone. It used to play with glasses
of the window thiking there was another bird.

KG

You know if you look at a window
pain, you would find yourself inside.

We had to be cutting its wing feather
so as not to fly. One day we forgot this
duty. The bird started a journey onto
the plains of Langata.

Both these birds, Kingstork and Minaba,
disappeared after learning to stay with
human beings.

MR. CANDLELIGHT'S HOUSE

At Naivasha there were farmers of the
same tribe with Mrs. Karen who could come
to visit Karen House, then called "Bogani
House". There were Mr. Moose candlelight
and Mr. "Samaki", so named due to his fondness
of eating fish, and Mr. Carl. They were brothers
all.

As I told Mrs. Karen, I was in need of
going to see the house of Mr. Candlelight
because he behaved as if this house was
better. Msabu told me I had to go with
the care of Mr. Pinja-Hatern driven by
Kinuthia. I carried my blankets and off

we went. Before entering the home we met Mr. and Mrs. Candlelight walking side by side. We passed warm greetings and they told us to be going to the house. We met Njuguna and Njoroge; well knowing we shook hands. Njuguna went to the kitchen, made tea and brought to us. We took and conversed.

Mr. Candlelight, who we all called "Kinyahwe", told Njuguna to give us a lot of food. They agreed there was a full leg of a sheep untouched and that would make enough meat for us both, with Kinuthia. Mr. Candlelight told us many nice things. He even said we should go with his wife that next day to me Mrs. Barance at the NAIROBI Show Grounds Sunday show.

The house was alright but it was not as good as Karen House.

CHILDREN OF THE BITCH RULE

MR. Ree and Mrs. Ree also did visit Karen house. They travelled from South Kinangop. I remember he carried my own brother Titi with two dogs to there home. Mrs. Karen said that Titi had to stay with Mr. Ree until she came back from Europe. Even the time Mrs. Karen went forever, she gave out the very two dogs to Mr. Ree. The dogs were "Curri" and "Dina", children of the bitch "Rule".

General Chui

MR. KAREN HE CRASHED

Mrs. Barance had no compromise with
her husband, Mr Barance BLixen, because
he was such an extravagant man. He left
out right for Tanganyika. One day he
came and demanded his wife to let me go
with him. Mrs. Barance refused with
distinctions. Insted he was given a Loud
dog to go with which was "Fence" by name.
She told him that I was her son. He was
told to carry another person to Arusha.
Mr. Karen crashed recently. I heard
he died in the crashing of his car.

"THE CLOCK ON TOP THE HOUSE"

Later there was put a clock on top the
house. The clock rang bells when it
reach anytime. Many children were coming
to listen to those bells. When Mrs. Karen
found them she could throw coins and sweets
to them. He who was not strong to collect
any coin was given sugar to make him happy.
There were many clocks inside the house,
even animal clocks, but the one on top
was the finest of all.

    This house of Mrs. Karen rang joy day
and night. Nobody felf sad. Even people
coming to the shamba could not say they
were going to the farm of a European. She
was of such good nature.

MZEE NUDESON HE MADE WHIPS

There was a poor old man who was first coming to Karen House one dawn and after reaching the verander he did sit on a chair. Then facing the clock and the flag, he started praying with his own Language. Mrs. Karen found him and opened the door for him. His house was near the old Karen stores and stable. Mrs. Karen told him to be coming daily with his basket for a bread and butter.

His only job was to make KIBOKO whips from wild skins. He was given by Mrs. Karen two Wakambas to be helping him in that Little business house.

Old Him was often a nusance because he would go to Nairobi and after managing to sell his whips, he could drink the whole Lot with strong drink in one day.

Mrs. Karen could not stay for two days without asking whether he had come for food. The man used to come with his basket and did sit on the verander. Mrs. Karen could order tea for both the two.

The Mzee stayed for three days without being seen at Karen. We never knew whether he was sick at Nairobi or what. He was expected to come the following day. The day passed and we found nobody.

On our way going inside the coffee Mrs. Karen found a sleeping figure. She asked me, Kamande, who is that? It seems as it is the poor old man. Is he sleeping or what is he doing? He never came for the bread, for we found his basket not far from him. All his things were scattered from him. Mrs. Karen asked is he alived? We started touching him here and there and we found him dead. His body was very much burnt by the heat of the sun.

Mrs. Karen said that he might have drunk a lot at Nairobi and he might have come on foot. She told me to be standing by the man, not to let anybody touch him. He was carried up to his little house and was lied on his bed. I was told to stay on a chair by the door, not let anybody inside, and to be feeling whether his heart might beat.   Later in the night Mrs. Karen returned with the Nairobi police and met me on the very chair.

They took the corpse of the old man with all his belongings. He was carried to Nairobi to be buried.

And thats all I can tell about that poor man who was given somewhere to stay by Mrs. Karen. I don't know how he was buried except I carried him to his house.   Mrs. Karen is the only person who knew his tribe.   Mrs Karen would call him " MZee Nudeson".

HER WHOLE ROOM FULL OF PICTURES AND BOOKS

Mrs. Karen sometimes was drawing pictures of people such as Nyeri Karuga, Muthuru Guthegu, and another Mzee known as Ireri. She called me and was telling me what she wanted of the people and I was to tell them each one to sit or do anything. She therefore did draw pictures for remembering our people all.

She would then go to the office and type a lot of papers. I never knew why or what she was intending to do with the whole room full of pictures and books. I would not ask her why she was doing so much. Even I never asked her which book she wanted to write. I was not knowing any of this.

"Look, Msabu . . . this is a good book.
It hangs together from the one end to the other.
Even if you hold it up and shake it strongly, it does not come to pieces.
The man who has written it is very clever.
But what you write . . . is some here and some there."

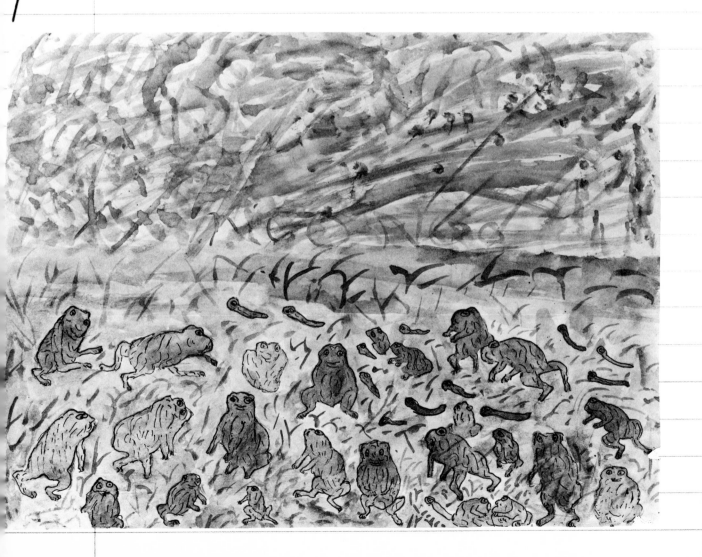

FARAH

LULU
and
ASKARI

LIONS FROM MASAI LAND

CHAPTER 13

Cattle killed ... Mr. Pinja-Hatern
and Mr. Thomas shoot lions in the coffee ...
two dead lions ... Matua meets his lion

"A lion-hunt each single time is an affair of perfect harmony, of deep,
burning, mutual desire and reverence between two truthful and undaunted creatures."

CHAPTER 13

LIONS FROM MASAI LAND

There has been coming Lions from Masai-Land and once they come upon two cattle. They came into the Karen cattle boma which shielded oxen. There the brave Lions, both males, slaughtered two cattle. They ate one and left the other. Early in the morning people found the cows eaten by Lions still fresh.

Mr. pinja-Hatern was present along with Mr. Thomas. Mr. Hatern was by then just off a journey of hunting animals. They told the people not to take anything from that half eaten cow till evening. In the evening Mr. Hatern and Mr. Thomas called all the people. A Lamp was given to Ali Mundigu to put on his head. pinja-Hatern had his hunter man in front of him. Mr. pinja-Hatern and Mr. Thomas were going to kill those Lions together with Said Kamau. This man belongs to the Muslims.

They started walking through the Lines of coffee where the Lions left the cows. Ali Mundigu was told to lead the battalion

in front. After a few minutes, he lit the
Lamp high on his head and the light of the
Lamp lighted the eyes of the Lions reflecting
each other. Then the Europeans hushed
Ali to stop as the Lions were nearly running.
Mr. Hatern shot at one of the Lions and the
light was put off. Ali was told to stand
steady. Then the light was put on again
and the other Lion looked. Mr. Thomas
shot it dead. People were warned not to
approach there, otherwise not being dead.
they would kill somebody. Pinja—Hatern
told his followers maybe there is another
Lion around so everybody should go home.
Early in the morning they all went to look
if the dead Lions were dead. Yes, the Lions
were very dead and they were carried to
Mrs. Baroness for slaughtering. She was
very interested in the two hides and two heads
for keeping in the house. Many people
took fat and the others took meat ... But
these Lions were killed because of eating
the cows of Mrs. Karen Blixen.
       One day another Lion had to kill. It
was coming from far off in Masailand. We

"Africa in flesh and blood"

took soda poison but it was not near by
enough. It stayed at the bounder of Mrs.
karen Blixen's. Another man, Kamba
in tribe, who was known as <u>Mutua</u>, had
gone to hunt for it with some others and
one European manager, who was known as
Mr. Rhino. Mutua saw the lion hidden in
a thicket. They all had guns.

"Lions, however, you might shoot at any time, within the distance of thirty miles to a farm."

Then Mutua thought of going near the thicket to see how the Lion entered in. By then the Lion had gone inside. He had turned head on the way, finally, so that when Mutua looked, he met face with this Lion. He Mutua had a gun with him but he could not move. Then the Lion went swop with a lot of bushes on the man. It lied on him. It tried to look for the man and the man was hidden underneath the bushes. So the other people shot it to death lying on the man and still the man couldn't move. Nobody wanted to go near it because then they thought it was not dead. By this time there was a certain boy who had a knife. He went step by step looking that Lion not wake up and kill them all. He met it dead. So Mutua was still with his gun, not harmed at all. The Lion was carried home and slaughtered.

I am experienced with only those three Lions which had brought troubles in Mrs. Karen's <u>shamba</u>. I have never heard or seen any other animal troubles in tha shamba apart from buffalos and monkeys which were many.

If there were Lion troubles they were killed by people beyond me.

"Very calm, with mighty paws . . . flows trouble the flowing grass, red-mouthed, silent, with the roar of the thunder ready in his chest."

"The views were immensely wide. Everything that you saw made for greatness
and freedom, and unequalled nobility."

MORE NGONG HUNTS LIKE BUFFALO
CHAPTER 14

I cook for the hunt…
I find strange beasts…Angata Rongai…
a snake 18 foot long

CHAPTER 14

More Ngong Hunts Like Buffalo

There is one day When Mrs. Karen and Mr. Thomas said that he had to go hunt up for buffalos just on Ngong Hills. We were thirteen Wakambas and I and Mr. Thomas Kinyanjui who went to trace the game. I Kamande was cooking morning meals when the buffalo was shot. The buffalo had a white spot on his stomach. Mr. Thomas was only interested with the head and the skin was given to Kinyanjui. Kinyanjui carried the skin and it was too heavy so he kept it in the home of a man who was known as Turugi Ngekenya. The wife of Kinyanjui carried the skin up to Karen store. Another time Mr. Thomas and Mrs. Karen said that they were to go with their dogs up to the home of a European as to get good buffalo.

The European was known as Mr. Tanner. We only slept for one

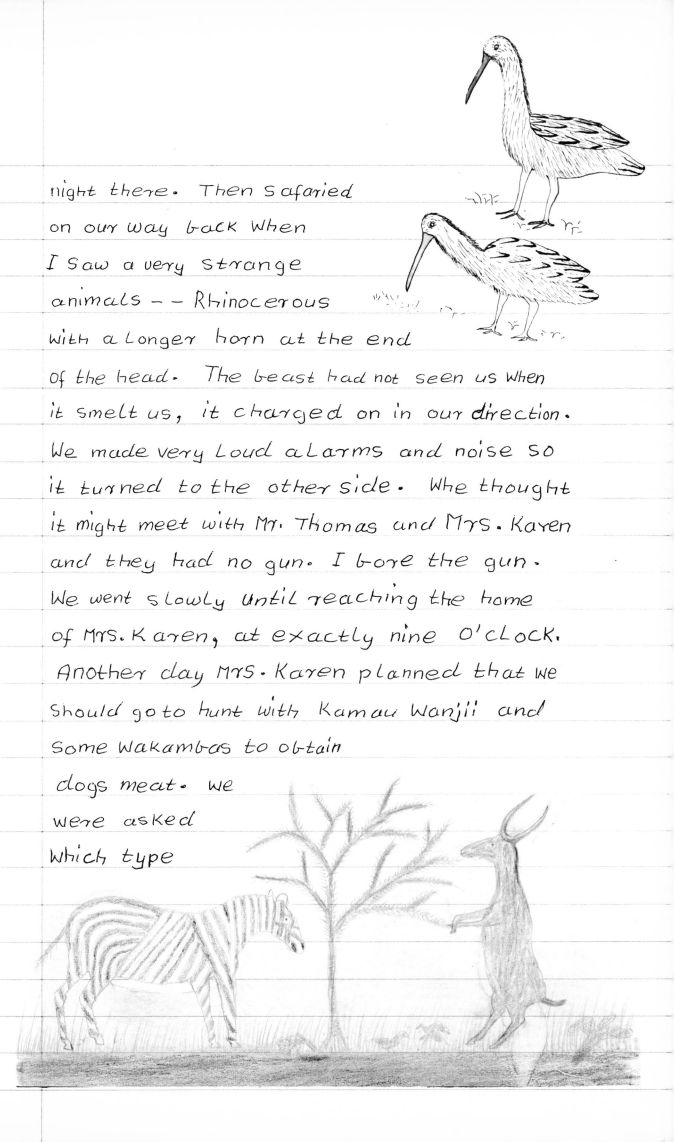

night there. Then safaried
on our way back When
I saw a very strange
animals - - Rhinocerous
with a longer horn at the end
of the head. The beast had not seen us when
it smelt us, it charged on in our direction.
We made very loud alarms and noise so
it turned to the other side. Whe thought
it might meet with Mr. Thomas and Mrs. Karen
and they had no gun. I bore the gun.
We went slowly until reaching the home
of Mrs. Karen, at exactly nine O'clock.
Another day Mrs. Karen planned that we
Should go to hunt with Kamau Wanjii and
Some Wakambas to obtain
dogs meat. We
were asked
Which type

of animal we like. Wakambas said they wanted zebra and we said we want a buck, for Kikuyu never eat zebras. The dogs ate zebras. So Mrs. Karen shot these two animals and two guinea fouls, the favored bird of Mrs. Karen... And I was given them to carry. The others were carrying meat for the dogs, and I and Kamau Wanjii followed Mrs. Karen on foot. We agin planned to go for a hunt to _Angata Rongai_ but we never gunned anything

because of a very big snake which was hanging on the tree. Mr. Thomas saw it first. We didn't know what the snake was waiting for.

The _Askari_ started to make noise and _Panya_ the dog started running forwards. We were told not to let _DUSK_ free otherwise it catches bad animals.

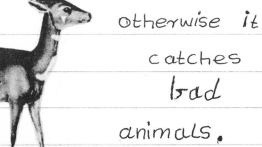

Ndongoro near Karen Farm
(Bongos)

At Ngong there were even giraffes, trimming the fields Dogs and peoples chased them however now they are none

Mr. Thomas went first and said this is a very big snake. The snake was shot three bullets on the head and was tied with rope and long stakes and carried home moving and afterwards slaughtered. Mr. Thomas was wanting only the skin, which salted at eighteen feet long. The skin was taken to Nairobi after it was dry. That day we never shot anything else edible because we became worried for the snakes were strange colourly and size.

That was my last time ever hunting.

Mr. Bror Blixen

the Top at Ngong

Mrs. Karen's Leopard

"I had seen the royal lion, before sunrise,
below a waning moon, crossing the grey plain on his way home from the kill,
drawing a dark wake in the silvery grass,
his face still red up to the ears, or during the midday-siesta,
when he reposed contentedly in the midst of his family. . . ."

"I came to look upon my acquaintance with the forest antelopes as upon a great boon, and a token of friendship from Africa."

"Lulu knew the place of the Giant Forest-Hog's lair and
had seen the Rhino copulate."

"No domestic animal can be as still as a wild animal.
The civilized people have lost the aptitude of stillness, and
must take lessons in silence from the wild before they are accepted by it."

 "Out in the wilds I had learned to beware of abrupt movements.
The creatures with which you are dealing there are shy and watchful,
they have a talent for evading you when you least expect it."

"The art of moving gently, without suddenness, is the first
to be studied by the hunter, and more so by the hunter with the camera."

"A herd of Elephant travelling...where the sunlight is strewn down...
pacing along as if they had an appointment at the end of the world"

"The elephant . . . in the course of time has adopted man
into his scheme of things, with deep distrust."

"A towering, overwhelming structure, massive as cast iron and little as running water"

I get the keys to the store . . .
I give medicine . . . responsibilities of the shamba . . .
one mistake in my service

"It was the upper mill-stone of the mill of the two murdered Indians. . . .
On the top side a pattern was carved, and it had a few large brown spots on it,
which my houseboys held to be the blood of the Indians, that would never come off.
The mill-stone table in a way constituted the centre of the farm."

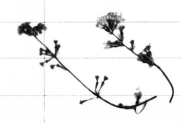

CHAPTER 15

My DOCTORSHIP

Mrs. Karen trust me very much that she would go to England and leave me with her dogs and the keys of the store where there were her possessions. I really could try with my level best keeping every place tidy.

The manager used to write her to overseas that everything did go okay and mostly the dogs; the dogs are even fatter than when she was present.

There used to come visitors and they were being told not to mind as I would provide them with anything available during the normal presence of Mrs. Karen.

Before leaving for anywhere, she used to tell me that when Chief Kinyanjui come for a visit, never wait. Do anything good. Give him beer and food, even meat. Entertain him as you can entertain your father. I had by then became a known cook. If European came, I could make cakes and call the houseboys to make Maggi soup.

When she was about to go to Europe,

She gave me a box of medicine and she told me that if anybody came sick either in the camp or from the shamba, I had to give them medicine. Tablets and drugs were in the box. Nobody was allowed to get the keys of the box. She left me the whole duty of the whole shamba people. Secondly, I was told that if I gave out the wrong medicine to a child or people, I would have God upon me. She told me that if there was any body sick she or he should come before 9 o'clock. It was only me being liable to give permission to go and sleep. He whom wasn't very ill, he had to go to work after my treatment. I was shown all the drugs of every sickness. I was to be staying in my house from morning till 9 o'clock awaiting anybody in trouble of injury, flu, or colds, or just to treat them. She told me that she never liked to hear any person say that he had taken the wrong medicine. I was to prevent children very much from getting into the store where the medicine was otherwise

Ali Khan's mules ("with one white horse")

"It was not I who was going away, I did not have it in my power to
leave Africa, but it was the country that was slowly and gravely withdrawing
from me, like the sea in ebb-tide."

he or she would chew the wrong drug. I
tried to obey her every word. But I never
could refuse to serve people even
at 10 o'clock. people could come even
during night time and call me for aid;
I couldn't rebuke them for calling me
when I was asleep. I woke up politely
to where danger or illness was. I went
on as a doctor for a very long time,
serving everybody.

I never did a mistake in my service
apart from one day I had asked for
a change to go and see my old stepbrother.
It was such a long time since we met
and talked. I went but my step-sister's
boy called Gatura caused trouble.
At the upper shamba, he was met by two
people. One person was my
stepbrother Ruhari. They
told Gatura that they had
come for treatment of
headaches both were
suffering. They asked
where I was and
were told that

Nairobi railroad station

En route to Europe

I had gone for a walk. Gatura took out the medicine; he said that he knew the headache tablets yet he took out the poison of washing cuts. The men were presented 2 doses. Ruhari never took his presently since he carried them with him. He passed to the younger wife of my father. After reaching he swallowed the poison with water. He began deadly ill. It started bursting his digestive organs. Luckily there was a river just by near, the very Athi river.

He started conducting the accute diahroe and vomiting as he ran to the water and drunk a lot of it and the breeze of the river helped. Kiguru (another brother) went and said that Ruhari was deadly sick and he had been given medicine by me. The car of Mrs. Karen was driven to look for me at Angata Rongai. In the car was Ali Hassan and Farah Aden. They met me and we drove back up to where Ruhari was. He was carried in the car with me up to Karen House. I started looking for eggs and milk as I was taught if anybody took

the wrong drug through mistake, I stirred
mebrance without yoke, adding milk, and told
him to drink. He became a bit better
from the stomache. That was the only
mistake in my doctorship. The man never
died.

Denys Finch-Hatton, last photo, Voi, 1931

"What business had I had ever to set my heart on Africa?"

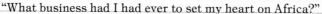

Denys Finch-Hatton and Karen

"I was up at great height, upon the roof of the world, a small figure in the tremendous retort of earth and air, yet one with it; I did not know that I was at the height and upon the roof of my own life."

E. Afr. Stan.
MAY 1931

THE VOI AIR TRAGEDY.

Machine Crashes After Taking-Off.

["STANDARD" CORRESPONDENT.]
London, May 15.

All the newspapers comment on the death of Hon. Denys Finch-Hatton, the "Times," publishing a column obituary notice. The Prince of Wales has expressed his sympathy with the Earl of Winchilsea.

Eye-Witness's Story

Further details of the air tragedy at Voi in which the Hon. Denys Finch-Hatton and his native Game Scout were both killed, have now been received in Nairobi.

An eye-witness of the disaster in a letter to Nairobi states that Mr. Finch-Hatton made a good take off and had risen well, heading in the direction of Nairobi, when the machine crashed. This witness of the accident who is a resident of Voi was the first person to reach the wreckage but was unable to get near to it as flames enveloped the whole machine, and the heat was intense. In his opinion both occupants of the machine must have been killed by the impact, rather than by the fire, as it was later found that the skulls of both men were badly fractured.

Trouble at Mombasa.

A Nairobi resident who was with Mr. Finch-Hatton at Mombasa, and later saw him at Voi, states that the machine left Mombasa on Tuesday. In endeavouring to take off from Mombasa one wheel ran into soft ground twice and Mr. Finch-Hatton is understood to have said that the machine very nearly overturned. On arrival at Voi Mr. Finch-Hatton discovered that one blade of his propeller was split in two places and from this he concluded that he must have struck the ground before leaving Mombasa.

Mr. Finch-Hatton telegraphed to Nairobi and a new propeller was sent to him. This he fitted on Wednesday morning. During Wednesday he took his Game Scout with him and they flew in the direction of Maktau. After flying for some time over the district a landing was made at a place about 12 miles south of Maktau station, as the Game Scout was not feeling well.

After a delay of about two hours a return flight was made to Voi where Mr. Finch-Hatton said that he had seen a herd of elephant on the Voi River.

Mr. Finch-Hatton spent Wednesday night at Voi and the flight which ended in disaster started early on Thursday morning.

THE FUNERAL.

A few hundred yards off the Kajiado Road in the Ngong Hills, overlooking the game reserve that stretched for miles below, the body of the Hon. Denys Finch-Hatton, M.C., was on Friday laid to rest in a simple grave and in the presence of friends and fellow-hunters.

No more appropriate place could have been chosen than this, a site on the edge of the game country which he had frequently traversed for the sake of observing the denizens of the reserve. The grave had been prepared just below the beacon on the Ngong Hills, some 20 miles from Nairobi, to which it was taken by motor hearse after having been brought up from Voi—the scene of his fatal crash in his aeroplane the day previous—to the capital by train.

The Mourners.

Over the same road in the afternoon came between 30 and 40 of his friends, comrades of the hunting profession, and others who had known and loved him. Over his remains was read the burial service by the Rev. G. B. Carlyle, Vicar of St. Mark's, Nairobi, until the appointed moment, when the

MR. PINJA-HATERN HOW HE GOT FIRE
CHAPTER 16

Mr. Pinja-Hatern flies away…elephants at Voi…
a new nose turner…the death of that man…
a lions' place in Ngong

"Death follows the happy man like a stern master,
The unfortunate like a servant. . . ."

CHAPTER 16

MR. PINJA-HATERN HOW HE GOT FIRE

Mr. pinja-Hatern had a small plane. He told Kinuthia and Hamisi that he had to go to Kilifi to his other shamba and also visiting elephant places by voi. Mr. pinja-Hatern told Kinuthia and Hamisi that they were to go with him. He had given them exactly their wages and Hamisi had not even divided some amounts for his wife.

They set off hurrying to the Nedge Road airport. After reaching, Hamisi asked him how they would go because he he had no clothes. He had only his Islam robe and no money inside. Kinuthia was ordered to take the car back to Mrs. Karen instead of going to Kilifi. Hamisi was told that he was to be given clothes from pinja's store. He then would go fly.

Kinuthia left Hamisi and Bwana Hatern on their way to Mombasa by plane. Hamisi's wife cried very hard but had nothing to do. Kinuthia took tea and left. He told Mrs. Karen that Mr. pinja-Hatern has left for mombasa with Hamisi alone.

HAMISI

...dead with
Mr. pinja-Hatern

The plane landed at Macknon Road and
also Kilifi... then Mombasa. This plane
was quite out of order. Pinja Tang to Nairobi
Airport for the engineer. The engineer
would send by train his new part, the
nose turner. The train started
leaving after dropping the new part and
the plane flew. Before even going for
about one mile, it got fire and crashed
down by voi station. The whole burned
at about eleven O'clock morning.

Mrs. Karen got the news of Mr. pinja-Hatern
and was very much worried. She told us that
she had to go to Nairobi for the details of
the news. Calling Farah and Kinuthia she
went. Before she left, she sent for Mr. Brucemis
to come and be in her home for the visitors who
would come. Mrs. Karen cried very much for
the death of that man. Many rich Europeans were
coming to do themselves danger for the pain
of that death. Many came to beseach
Mrs not to do harm to herself, for death
is awaiting everyone.

She said that he was not to be burried
either in Nairobi or where he died.

He was to be carried in a coffin and to be burried at Kandisi, a lions' place in her Ngong Farm. But there was rains to hinder the Idea.

They were very Long friends and they Liked each other. He Liked to go outside very many times and could stay in the forest for even a year. people could think he was dead in the wildlife. Before he was dead he was saying he would Like to be burried at Kandisi. And indeed Mrs. Karen herself wanted to be burried there.

"He prayeth well, who loveth well
Both man and bird and beast."

HOW MR DINJA-HATERN SEES ALL
KAREN HOUSE 1931

THE FABLES
FROM KAREN FARM DAYS

1. The Sour grapes of the Fox
2. The Ape and the Dolphin
3. An Ox and A Big Frog
4. A Fly in the pot
5. The Crane and the Swan's Song
6. The Rat, the Frog, and the Hawk
7. THE Ant and the grasshopper
8. an ass and a Wild pig
9. The Snake and the File
10. The Lion and the Mouse
11. The Frogs who Demanded a King
12. The Dog and his Shadow
13. The Black Bird and the jug
14. The Hyaena and the Lion
15. The Jackal and the Vulture
16. The Antelop, the Monkey, the Leopard
17. The Lion the Bird and the Gazelle
18. The Monkey and the Lion
19. The Leopard Without a tail
20. The Tortoise and the Hare
21. The FIGHT OF THE FOREST

THE SOUR GRAPES OF THE FOX

A fox looked and beheld the grapes that grew upon a tall vine, which grapes he much desired.

And when he saw that he might get none he turned his sorrow into joy saying"... "These grapes are sour, and I had some I would not eat them."

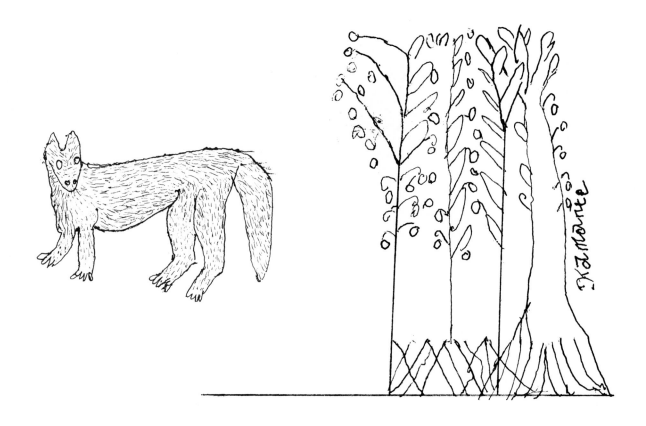

HE IS WISE WHO PRETENDS NOT TO DESIRE THOSE WHICH HE MAY NOT HAVE

THE ape and the DOlphin
Nyani na Samaki (POMBO)

Far away Sailors were wanting ~~the~~ apes and animal children
to amuse the dull time on board ships. When off a far coast a ship
Carrying an ape turned over in heavy stormwater; everybody
droped in the ~~deep~~. As it happened; nearby was a famous
city; and everybody ~~stu~~ Struggled in the water towad the city.
And the ape strugguled only failing
by his lack in swiming education.
With great ~~book~~ luck a dolphin
fish arose
beside him and
~~S~~ Seeing him for
a man took him
on his back

When they finished
miles of swinning
and entered into the
gate of the port
Called MOMBASA,
the dolphin asked
of his passanger;
"Do you know
'MOMBASA' well?"
"Very naturally";
Said the ape;
"and very well; for he is an old
friend of the family...There never lived anyone
so pleasant"; he continued. "Well friend, you are a bit
Of a villain"; Said the dolphin, and he dived down
with his burden at once in a wave.

MOMBASA

PRIDE BEFORE
A FALL
KIBURI Mbele ya Kuanguka

AN OX AND A BIG FROG

The frog and her family of frog children had an ox come upon their pond water one morning. In her great pride the frog mother swelled up inside against the ox and asked her children if she was not as great as the ox and mighty. "No mother" they groaned together, "next to the ox you are almost nothing". And the frog mother took another great breath inside saying with difficulties, "Am I not now more mighty?"

"<u>NO</u>," groaned the frog children together, "the ox here <u>is the biggest in the World</u>".

And the frog mother took in more air than ever and was about to say something when she popped. And she Lay exploded on the ground.

A FLY IN THE POT

A fly than Landed into a pot of meat saw her leg sticking in sauce. Knowing she would not breathe Long in the boiling air, she said out Loud, "Oh, I have drunk so much and eaten so much and Lived so much I may dies rightfully ~~fall~~ fed".

A WISE MAN BEARS WITH MIGHTY COURAGE THAT THING THAT CAN IN NO WAY BE AVOIDED.

THE CRANE AND THE SWAN'S SONG

A crane was attracted at the curious light song of a dying swan and came to tell her it was against nature to sing at such a time. " Why? ", asked the swan, " I am entering astate of quiet and ended danger without guns or snares or hunger. I will not tire or be afraid and who would not show joy at this delivering? "

DEATH BEING ONLy A LAST FAREWELL TO DIFFICULTIES AND PAIN.

THE RAT, THE FROG AND THE HAWK (Panya na chura na Mwéwé)

A rat started a long voyage toward the distance
and after some days he was made to stop by a river.
He found a frog and so sought him out saying
"Sir frog in my voyage I must get over the river."
The frog with a broad smile showed him
a fast swimming lesson with all his skills.
Then the rat allowed the master swimmer to bind
together their legs with a cord...And they
thus went into the exact middle of the river.
And as they were there the clever frog stood still
to the end that the rat should scream and go
down. And yet before anything took place a hawk
flew nearby and spied the two meals
tied together and he grabbed them
in his two claws and took them
to the far edge of the river
and ate them wet.

HE WHO THINKS EVIL AGAINST GOOD,
THE EVIL HE THINKS WILL FALL
TO HIM

(afikiriaε mbaya ni mzuri
mbaya tangūkia yéyé)

THE ANT AND GRASSHOPPER

A starved grasshopper in the Winter rains went and demanded of the ant her corn to eat. And then the ant said to the grasshopper, "What have you done all the summer past?", and the grasshopper answered, "I have sung". And after that the ant said, " Of my corn you shall have none, as you have sung summer, dance now in winter".

THERE IS A TIME TO DO LABOUR AND WORK, AND TIME TO REST. HE THAT DOES NOT WORK SHALL HAVE AT HIS TEETH GREAT COLD, AND LACK OF HIS NEED.

AN ASS AND A WILD PIG

An ass was making jokes of a pig
diging roots in his field. At length
this pig Looked up from his work
and said, "Dull ass, as it is you
please joke on! The world can see
the smallness of you that protects
you well against my easy revenge."

DO NOT GET ENRAGED
AT DULL REMARKS —
UNTRUTH MAY GAIN
    TRUTH

THE SNAKE AND THE FILE

The Snake has always felt anger against the file because long ago when it was dying of hunger it addressed a file for the favour of a meal. How stupid you must be", Said the file, "to imagine getting anything from me who always takes from everyone and never gives anything in return".

The Snake Seized the file and gnawed and chewed it until the file said, " Rage and vanity are dulling your teeth. You wear away, but not me, For I daily chew brass and steel and have little dread of your soft grinders".

BE CAUTIOUS WHOM you ENGAGE
ENERGY BEING EASILY MISSPENT

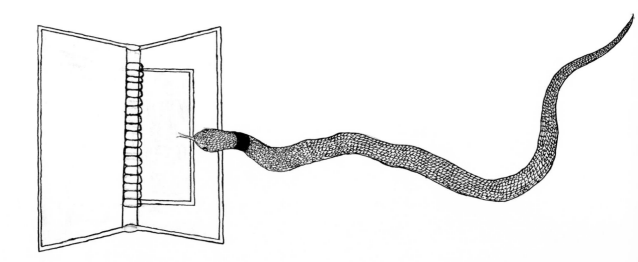

THE LION AND THE MOUSE

Upon the huge roaring of a beast in the wood, a mouse ran presently out to see the news; and what was it but a lion hampered by the hunter's net.

Only days before the mouse had been delivered from under the paw of a certain generous lion and the memory was strong. A strict inquiry into the news of the hunter's net and the mouse found to her amezement the very lion, her friend. and set to work henceforth upon the couplings of the net gnawing them into pieces and readily her preserver.

THE GREAT AND THE LITTLE
NEED EACH OTHER

THE FROGS WHO DEMANDED A KING

There were frogs which were in ditches and ponds in their freedom. And then one day all of one assent and of one will they called up to God that he would give them a King. God was not pleased with this, but seeing how simple the frogs were, He soon sent down a log of wood into the water with great noise, Whereby all the frogs were afraid and dreaded the Log. Some time after they slowly gathered up closser to proclaim their respect of obedience. But nothing took place and soon Later the frogs perceived it only was a piece of wood, their King, and they squatted on it.   So they turned to God again praying him sweetly that He would give them another King. God was once more unpleased and soon He sent down to them a heron for their King.   The heron King stood in the water and ate one frog after the other when the frogs saw their King eating them in a line, fiercely, they

began tenderly to weep, saying in this way to God — Mighty sir, and right high God of all, please deliver us and God called down to them, "The king which you demanded is your master. When men have what they ought to have they ought to be happy. He that has Liberty ought to keep it well and not make demands!"

LIBERTY SHOULD NOT BE
SOLD FOR ALL THE
GOLD AND SILVER
IN THE WORLD

THE DOG AND HIS SHADOW

In time past was a dog returning to his village a long a river, and he held in his mouth large slices of meat. As he passed by a place near river water he saw reflections of hanging down meat in a dog's mouth —

— thinking it was another slice of meat, he opened his mouth to grab it. Down fell his meal into the current.

HE THAT WANTS ANOTHER MAN'S GOOD OFTEN LOSSES HIS OWN.

THE BLACK BIRD AND THE JUG

A black bird ready to die of thirst beheld a jug. He glided to it without delay and indeed found water in it. With much strain and reaching on his neck he found the water beyond his reaching, so far away was it at the bottom. He made efforts toward overturning the jug in the hopes of just a piece, but no it was heavy.

Resting at last with sad eyes, he stared at the ground. On each side of him, indeed, were assembled light pebbles. Taking them into his beak he cast them to the bottom of the jug, where being the water grew higher and higher by degrees. In time it grew to the very edge of the jug and, rewarded, the black bird drank his desire.

DESPAIR AND FORCE LOSE
BEFORE INVENTION
AND INDUSTRY

THE ANTELOPE, THE MONKEY, the LEOPARD

An antelope, in the presence of a leopard, demanded of a monkey a bushel of roots and fruit. And the leopard commanded the monkey to pay it. And when the payment day arose, the antelope came to the monkey and demanded his roots and fruit. And the monkey from a high branch said to him, " Covenants and pacts made by dread and force are not holding.

SOMETIMES IS NECESSARY TO PROMISE SOMETHING TO AVOID GREAT DAMAGE AND LOSS. THINGS DONE BY FORCE HAVE NO MEANING.

THE LION, THE BIRD AND THE GAZELLE

A Lion found himself a guinea hen and was preparing to devour it when he caught sight of a gazelle hurrying by. Leaving the bird and at a great pace he leapt toward the new gazelle. But all too late and his distance became wide in the escap. Turning again to guinea hen the Lion found it too had gone.

A BIRD IN THE HAND IS WORTH TWO IN THE BUSH

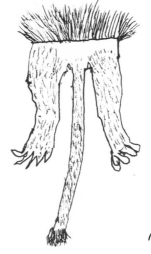

THE MONKEY AND THE LION

The monkey made a grand impression by dancing
before an assembly of animals who thereby elected
him King. The Lion was jealously
Remembering a snare with food in it, &
he addressed the King to inform him
of a choice morsel which, instead of
eating it himself, he had saved for the royal
office. And the monkey
swallowed this bait and
found himself snared and soon
called the lion to blame   who
replied. "Fancy a fool like you   ,friend,
monkey, being King of the
animals."

ATTEMPT BEYOND
YOUR POWER &
COURT MISFORTUNE.

Kamante AND Njuguna s/o Kamande

A sly old Leopard nevertheless found himself victim in a hunter's trap one night with no moon. Before getting a way out he lost his tail. He became so awkward and ashamed he summoned a meeting of all the Leopards. With his back to a tree he spoke as follows:— "Dear brother Leopards, by consideration of the worth of our long tails, I come upon a conclusion that we become smarter without them. They drag us down behind and sweep the mud and catch thorns and serve us no purpose. So upon my word it is our duty we cut them off now and for all".

THE LEOPARD WITHOUT A TAIL

"Well spoken", replied a wise Leopard in the council, "there may yet be something to your words. Could we first ask you to turn around from the tree?" A storm of laughter shook the council hailing this turn of events, and Long leopard tails forever after were in.

MISERY WANTS COMPANY.

By Kamande
Gatura

THE TORTOISE AND THE HARE

A sleek hare found himself very fond of mocking the tortoise about slow walking. And as he talked and laughed he jumped backwards and forwards in the flashing of and eye. The tortoise at some length smiled and said, "Yes", that a race should become scheduled. " Any time any place", laughed the quick hare.

On the morning of the great race, a mole judge pointed the starting gun. The tortoise waited earnestly at the line. The hare sat behind on the edge of the road eating carrots and a cabbage, smiling to his friends. When the race gun started, the tortoise plodded on his way down the road but the hare, full knowing his speed, decided on waiting a bit to finish his vegetables in front of his friends. They marvelled and admired him. And the tortoise had gone on the routed plodding a straight line step . after step, and they saw him there slowly on his way.

After a time and when the last carrot was gone the hare waved to his friends and ran with high jumps down the road. It was a day of great sunlight and soon the high stepping rabbit said to himself that he might just lie down a little under the shade. And he did it after a yawn. And he had left the tortoise far behind, and he lay fast asleep.

Meanwhile, and even despite the sun throughout the day, the tortoise plodded on his route. As he looked only forward he did not see the hare fast asleep under the shade bush when he passed. Nearing the evening when the sun turned into its red colour, with a jump the hare ran to his feet and seeing the time, fled at great urgent leaps for the finish line in a panic. As the fat and red sun reached over west horizons so did the hare in his stride, exhausted, to find the finish line and the judge mole and the tortoise patiently waiting there.

SLOWLY AND STEADY WINS THE RACE.

FIGHT OF THE FOREST

Once upon a time there was a friendly Kings, King Bongo and King Kudu. Every King was telling the other one is greater than the other, because they were living both at the great forest.

One day When they were competiting, they promised to fight and who is to win is a king of the earth and who is defeated is a king of the heaven. And at the very moment it broke a fight, both they fought and fought from sun rise to the sun set.

And while they were fighting they ran up to a big tree fallen down. As he always does, King Bongo went underneath. And as he always does King Kudu jumped over. Well King Bongo stretched his head and sting King Kudu stomach who shouted, I am defeated, defeated! defeated.!!!.

And King Bongo told him, from now onward be living on mountains and I live on lowlands and great forests.

OUT OF AFRICA
Karen Blixen, 1915

Above the glaring street lamps, quietly keeping watch,
The moon wanders forth tonight in clouds and mist.
Long do I stare at the moon to know her once more,
As I watched her in the old days, wondering now if she can see,
The shadows of haze over Longonot,
Where the long slope follows the edge of the plain . . .
Wondering if she can see herself mirrored in the waves of Guaso Nyiro,
Beyond Kijabe and Ngong,
To my free land, my endless land, my heart's terrain.
Where the sign of the Southern Cross
Stands above the wasteland of the plains . . .
The plains of the great mirages,
In the Masai Reserve.

Returning from a hunt, I recall the sweet fragrance of the grass
And smoke rising from my campfire into the pale air of twilight.
When putting game on the spits to roast, Ismael told hunting stories . . .
Love stories from another age;
Sabagathi brought firewood, Farah put my gun away and served us wine.
In the cool, blue night long sparks shot out . . .
Many things come and go in the embers of the campfire.
And when I turned my eyes toward the darkness of night
I saw you, silent moon, high in your loneliness,
Shining down as you moved forward on your vigil
On the hunting lions, on the plains of gentle evenings,
In the Masai Reserve.

a strange view of the Ngong Hills 1921

In the clear tropical darkness, whose majesty was never touched
Before the white people came, I hear sounds that die and reoccur,
As the night wind runs, runs without rest, a thousand miles through grass and thorn.
And in moonlight on the iron-grey plains
Zebra herds graze, small spots of light . . .
Like tears on the cheeks shooting stars run down the sky and disappear.
Millions of insects moan in song;
Then the old voice of the plain thunders through the dark . . .
Never forgotten when once heard, stirring everyone's blood,
Echoing near and far.
It is the lions hunting. In the vast moonlit nights,
In the Masai Reserve.

When the stars tremble, growing pale on the sky's breast,
And hill and valley shimmer from the dew,
The lions leave their kill, glancing eastward
And amble homeward in cold opal mist.
Silent in the dawn sky flight after flight of geese pass by,
Eland and zebra move through the silvery waves of grass,
And from a circle in the Masai manjatta smoke drifts away at a great distance,
And the young girls, gazelle-eyed, open the wattle gates for their cattle,
Counting and content as they file out . . .
In the cold air their sheep are bleating,
On the plains in the clear mornings,
In the Masai Reserve.

RUNGSTEDLUND
Rungsted Kyst   19 July, 1962

My good and faithful servant Kamande,

    I was glad to get your letter with the two photos
and to learn that you and your family are well. I was
also glad to hear about you from Mr. Peter Beard, and
I wish I had been with you to my old house, so that we
could talk of old days.
    I am sending you a small present of money to help
you a little in the bad times.
    I am still living in the old house where I was born.
It is very lovely here, and I am well.
    Mr. Thomas is well, and he asks me to send you his
greetings. He has got four children and six grandchildren.. He is living not far from me.
    I pray to God that you may be well, and that your
children and your whole family may be in good health
and have good luck. I wish that I could see you again.
    So goodbye, Kamande.

                    Baroness Blixen,

Dear Kamante Gatura —

    I would like to tell you how much the world that you are a part of, so far away in Kenya, means to us in the United States, through the writings of your "parent", Baroness Karen Blixen.

    I have read all her books — and about you in them.

    Now Peter Beard has shown me your book. It is most wonderful. It makes me wish that I knew your country and your life. I have read it to my children. Each evening they ask me to read it again.

    My son, John, loves the stories about animals and the pictures. With this letter I am sending you a picture he drew for you.

    Do you know what Peter Beard said to me about your book when he gave it to me? He said, Kamante's memories of Karen Blixen are so beautiful... If she were able to see it, it would be the deepest, highest echo she could have longed for. Yes, at last Africa has a song for her. Yes, I'm sure the eagles of the Ngong hills look out for her.

    Those were my thoughts too, when I had finished your book. It must make you proud and happy that you have made such a memorial to her.

    My nephew, Robert Kennedy jr, has told us of his pleasure in meeting you. He has told us how he loved playing with the monkey Northichongo, and the wart hogs.

    I am sending you a picture of President Kennedy. I hope one day to bring his children to Kenya, and to find you there.

    May I ask you to sign these 2 pictures of yourself for my children, Caroline and John? I would be most grateful.

    Please extend my best regards to your wife Wambui, and to your brother and your sons.

Most Sincerely

Jacqueline Kennedy

DEAR Jacquelie Kennedy

I am very glad to indicate these few lines for greetings to you; how are you since I have received your wards on it, I was very sorry to hear since Last year act. I have been sending your letters, but none of them you received, I hope this time you have to get this one with some drawings in it.

I also happy to see your photographs and your children again it gives me much presure to hear to meet peter Beard and you are all together talking something concerning me and talking how you will came one day in Kenya, I hope if God wishes and if all goes well we shall meet here Nairobi, that time we shall greet each other, talking about my hopes and my dreams and fill as I was filling during I was meeting with MRS Baroness BLixen

As she Left peter Beard as my brother because, she send peter to came and Look me wheather I died during Kenya imagenice; and he came alright and met me at mine, and told me he was send by Karen to see me, We greet each other and then he went back to Denmark, where he went to see Karen, after a short time he send me aletter that Karen has died; from there and there I was very astonished, so up to now MR peter is my brother wheather he is in America or here in Kenya, because I am with him now and then.

I pray God to keep you together up to date both MR peter and your children, I also very glad for remembering to send me aletter also I am so far from you. Therefore I hope to Keep the friendship between you and your family untill we meet all together here in Kenya, pass my best wishes greeting to your family from my wife wambui and my children. God may bless you many days. YOURS — KAMANEE gatoRa

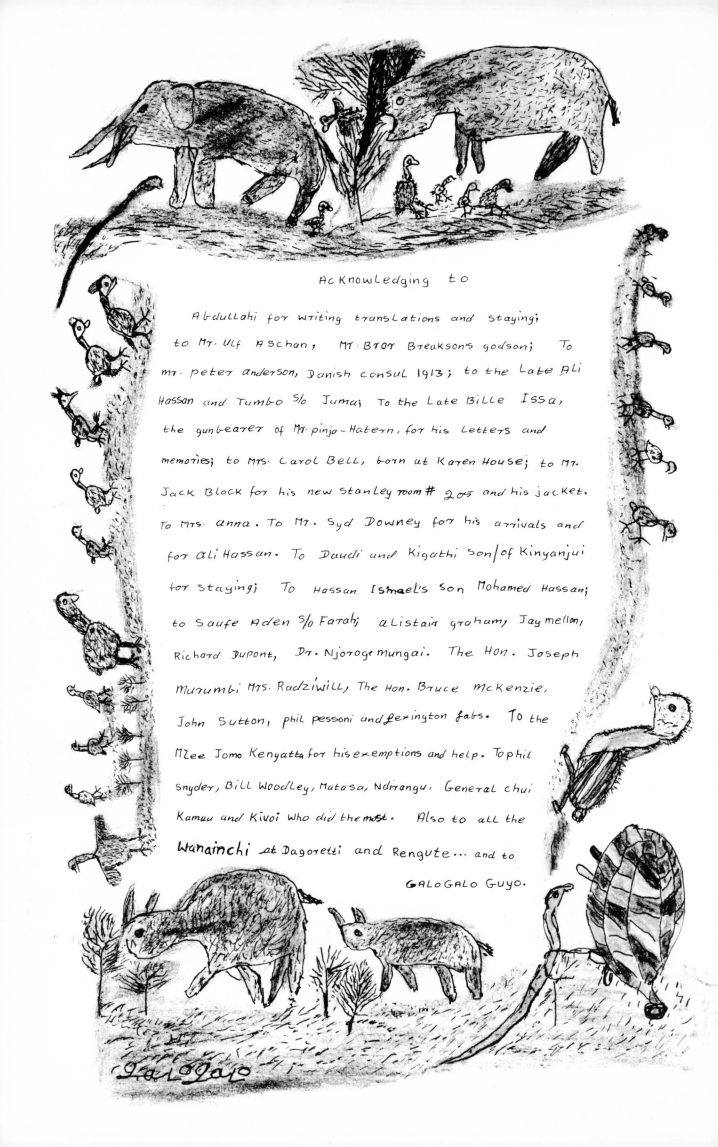

Acknowledging to

Abdullahi for writing translations and staying; to Mr. Ulf Aschan, Mr. Bror Breakson's godson; To Mr. peter anderson, Danish consul 1913; to the Late Ali Hassan and Tumbo S/o Juma; To the Late Bille Issa, the gunbearer of Mr. pinja-Hatern, for his Letters and memories; to Mrs. Carol Bell, born at Karen House; to Mr. Jack Block for his new stanley room # 205 and his jacket. To Mrs. anna. To Mr. Syd Downey for his arrivals and for ali Hassan. To Daudi and Kigathi son/of Kinyanjui for staying; To Hassan Ismael's Son Mohamed Hassan; to Saufe Aden S/o Farah; alistair graham, Jay mellon, Richard Dupont, Dr. Njoroge mungai. The Hon. Joseph Murumbi Mrs. Radziwill, The Hon. Bruce McKenzie, John Sutton, phil pessoni and Lexington Labs. To the Mzee Jomo Kenyatta for his exemptions and help. To phil snyder, Bill Woodley, Matasa, Ndirangu, General chui Kamau and Kivoi who did the most. Also to all the Wanainchi at Dagoretti and Rengute... and to GALOGALO Guyo.

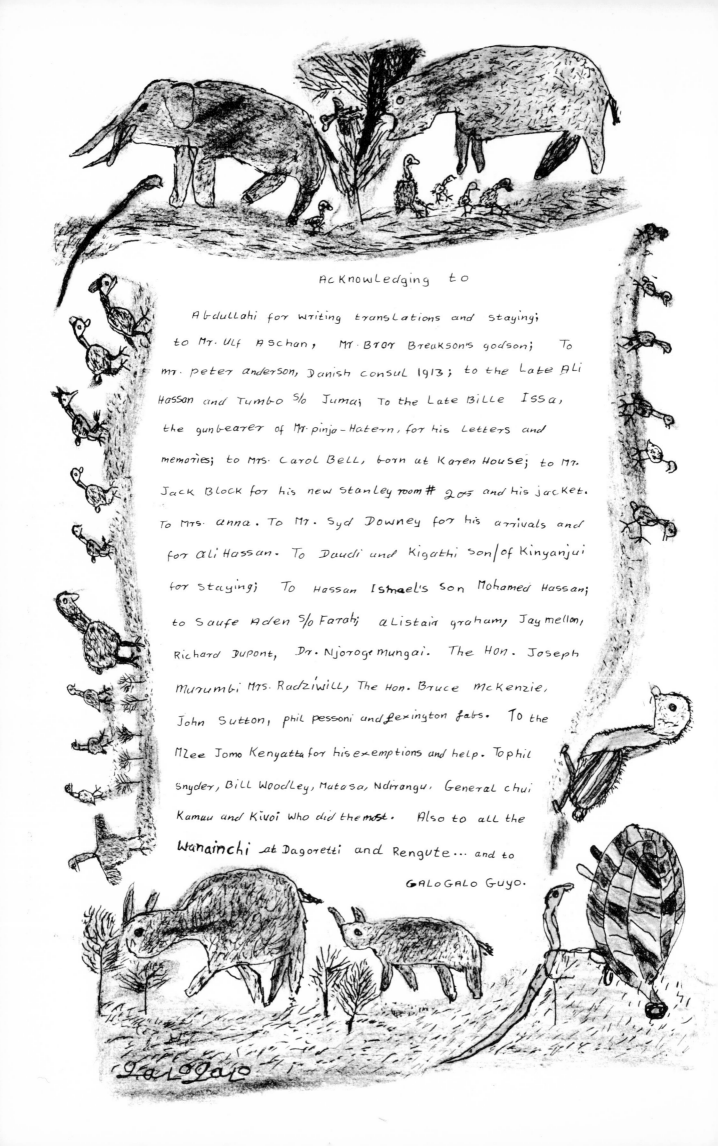

Acknowledging to

Abdullahi for writing translations and staying;
to Mr. Ulf Aschan, Mr. Bror Breakson's godson; To
Mr. Peter Anderson, Danish consul 1913; to the Late Ali
Hassan and Tumbo S/o Juma; To the Late Bille Issa,
the gunbearer of Mr. Pinja-Hatern, for his letters and
memories; to Mrs. Carol Bell, born at Karen House; to Mr.
Jack Block for his new Stanley room # 205 and his jacket.
To Mrs. Anna. To Mr. Syd Downey for his arrivals and
for Ali Hassan. To Daudi and Kigathi son/of Kinyanjui
for staying; To Hassan Ismael's son Mohamed Hassan;
to Saufe Aden S/o Farah; Alistair graham, Jay mellon,
Richard Dupont, Dr. Njoroge Mungai. The Hon. Joseph
Murumbi Mrs. Radziwill, The Hon. Bruce McKenzie,
John Sutton, Phil Pessoni and Lexington Labs. To the
Mzee Jomo Kenyatta for his exemptions and help. To Phil
Snyder, Bill Woodley, Matasa, Ndirangu, General Chui
Kamau and Kivoi who did the most. Also to all the
Wanainchi at Dagoretti and Rengute... and to
GALOGALO GUYO.

The following people on three continents have helped to make this book: in Africa, the Blocks, General Chui, Kamante's three sons Njuguna, Simon, and Francis Gatura, Galo Galo Guyo, Harry Horn, Matasa Isaya, Nathaniel Kivoi, Ingrid Lindstrom (above left), Charles Njonjo, Monty and Hilary Ruben, Murray Watson, and Bill and Ruth Woodley; in Denmark, the entire Dinesen family, the Keith Kellers, Eric and Anne Kopp, the Royal Library of Copenhagen, the Rungstedlund Foundation, and Clara Svendsen; in New York, Steven M. L. Aronson, Eugene Gordon, Kay Lee, Roberta Leighton, Mike Miller, Betty Paul, Kathy Robbins, Bettina Rossner, Arnold Skolnick, and Anne T. Zaroff at Harcourt Brace Jovanovich, Ben Albala, Henry Austin, Joe Behar, Elaine Donnelly, Helen Earle, Hoyt Evans, Rod Leprine, Peter Nassau, Tom O'Brien, Lou Portella, Sid Rapoport, and Sam Schiff at Rapoport Printers, and Barbara Allen, Alison Bond, and Helen Merrill.

"Now all is done that could be done.
And all is done in vain."
Shadows on the grass

What an extraordinary surprise and gift it was, when Peter Beard first showed me the fables and drawings of Isak Dinesen's beloved Kamante. I had not known he was still alive. To hold his drawings was like touching a talisman that took you back to a world you thought had disappeared forever.

Maybe I was so affected because Out of Africa has always meant more to me than any other book. But then I watched my children responding to the fables with the freshness of young minds. My son started to make African drawings, some of which he asked Peter Beard to send to Kamante for him.

Thomas Dinesen's introduction to the first section of this book is of historical importance. He is that stoic figure standing so straight in the snow on Mount Kenya. What homage it does him. He was a hero. He reflects the tradition of his sister; one of highest discipline. Isak Dinesen, Baroness Blixen, had her special views about the aristocracy. She felt that the noble spirit was the true aristocrat. She said aristocrats were not more virtuous than other people — "what they had above all was courage, and after that, taste and responsibility — and endurance."

Peter Beard reveals the immediacy her philosophy can have for the young people of today — who are so passionately idealistic, so ready to be martyrs. This book can help them; show them that they had allies in an earlier time, who knew that courage was endurance as well as abandon.

Today, everything is about to happen. But "about" can mean a generation, not the next six months. That is where the courage of endurance comes in. Black people, here as well as in Africa, know what endurance means. Isak and Thomas Dinesen knew too.

How contemporary Isak Dinesen is; her prescience of how man would destroy his environment, her belief that his only hope was to get in tune with it again. It seems to me that so many of the movements of today, ecology, anti-materialism, communal living — they were all in Out of Africa.

She was one of the first white people to feel that "black is beautiful." She was the first to see how "all the dark forces of time, evolution, nature" were being disrupted in Africa. Cecil Rhodes saying "teach the native to want" so quickly became Galbraith's "Affluent Society."

One of my favorite passages in Out of Africa is where Isak Dinesen asks: "If I know a song of Africa, of the giraffe and the African new moon lying on her back, of the ploughs in the fields and the sweaty faces of the coffee pickers, does Africa know a song of me? Would the air over the plain quiver with a color that I had had on, or the children invent a game in which my name was, or the full moon throw a shadow over the gravel of the drive that was like me, or would the eagles of the Ngong Hills look out for me?"

This book is the echo she longed for. Yes, Africa does have a song for her. It is Peter Beard and Kamante who have made it for her.

Kamante's drawings and Peter Beard's photographs share a purity — of a wild animal looking at the camera with free and vulnerable eyes.

This book is a work of love — of a love that a young man, young enough to be her grandson, was struck with when he first read Out of Africa. That book changed his life. He went in search of that Africa she knew. He saved its' memories, her memories, for us.

Before it is too late?

Jacqueline Bouvier Onassis
Montauk June 1